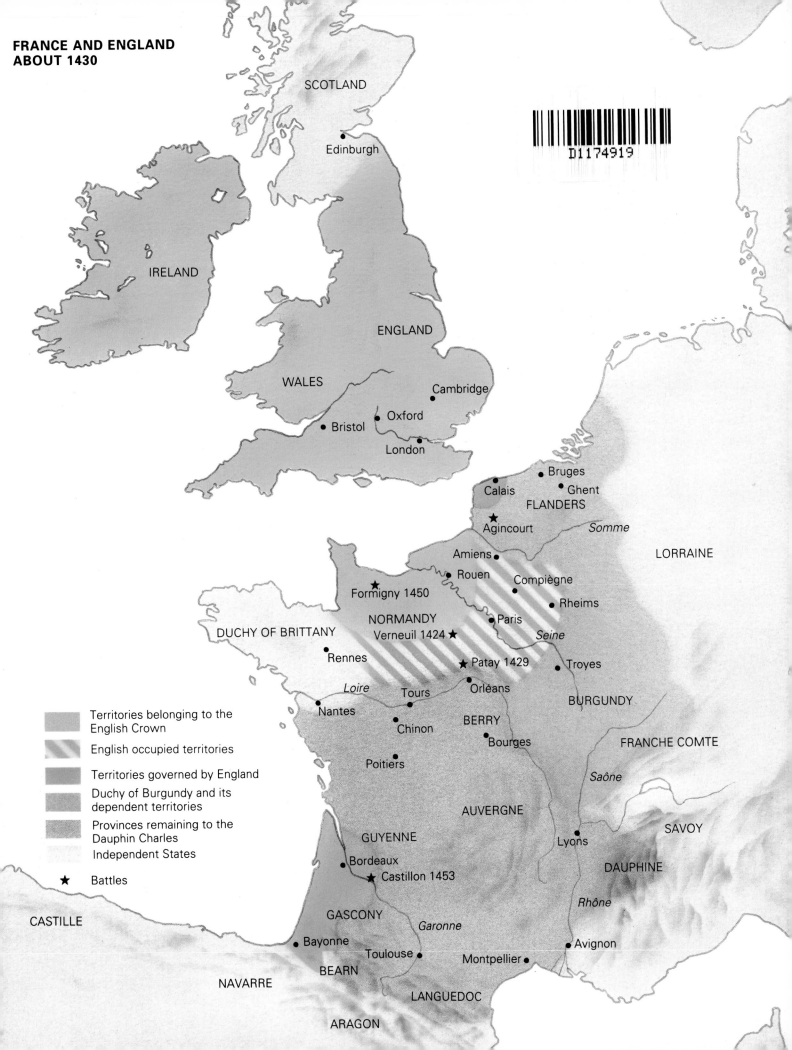

FRANCE AND ENGLAND
ABOUT 1430

SCOTLAND

Edinburgh

IRELAND

ENGLAND

WALES

Cambridge

Oxford

Bristol

London

Bruges

Calais
Ghent

FLANDERS

Agincourt
Somme

Amiens
LORRAINE

Rouen
Compiègne

Formigny 1450
Rheims

NORMANDY
Paris

DUCHY OF BRITTANY
Verneuil 1424
Seine

Rennes
Patay 1429
Troyes

Loire
Tours
Orléans
BURGUNDY

Nantes
BERRY
FRANCHE COMTE

Chinon
Bourges

Poitiers
Saône

AUVERGNE
SAVOY

GUYENNE
Lyons

Bordeaux
DAUPHINE

Castillon 1453

Rhône

GASCONY
Garonne
Avignon

CASTILLE
Bayonne

Toulouse
Montpellier

BEARN

NAVARRE
LANGUEDOC

ARAGON

Territories belonging to the
English Crown

English occupied territories

Territories governed by England

Duchy of Burgundy and its
dependent territories

Provinces remaining to the
Dauphin Charles

Independent States

★ Battles

Contents

Published by Evans Brothers Limited
2A Portman Mansions
Chiltern Street
London W1M 1LE

Copyright © 1990 Casterman, originally published
in French under the title Les Jours de l'Histoire:
La Guerre de Cent Ans

English translation copyright
© Evans Brothers Limited 1993

English translation by arrangement with
Bookdeals Translations
PO Box 263
Taunton TA3 6RH
UK

Maps by Michael Welply

Published by agreement with Casterman, Belgium

All Rights Reserved. Without limiting the rights
under copyright reserved above, no part of this
publication may be reproduced, stored in a
retrieval system or transmitted in any form or by
any means electronic, mechanical, photocopying,
recording or otherwise, without prior permission
of Evans Brothers Limited.

Printed in Hong Kong by Dah Hua Printing Co. Ltd.

ISBN 0 237 51279 3

EVANS HISTORY LIBRARY

THE HUNDRED YEARS WAR

Lionel Dumarche and Jean Pouëssel
English translation by Anton Wills-Eve
Illustrations by Morgan

Evans Brothers Limited

Foreword

The Battle of Cocherel, May 16, 1364. Illumination from Froissart's chronicles, fifteenth century. (Bibliothèque Nationale, Paris.)

I t was not until the nineteenth century that historians first called the conflict between England and France in the late Middle Ages "The Hundred Years War". This was a convenient title for a war which had no specific beginning or end but lasted at least 116 years, from 1337 to 1453. Some historians put the dates even further apart, from the first annexation of Guyenne in 1294 to the peace of Picquigny in 1475. According to them, the Hundred Years War would have lasted some 180 years! But whatever dates are taken, it is important to remember that the fighting was not continuous. There were breaks; sometimes short cease-fires of a few weeks or months, sometimes truces or peace agreements lasting several years. Another important point is that all the fighting took place on the continent. Indeed, with the exception of a few coastal raids, none of the fighting took place on English soil, whereas the whole of France was at some time a battleground. Largely for diplomatic reasons, the war also affected all the countries bordering France and England in the fourteenth century, from Spain in the south to Scotland in the north. To the east Alsace, Lorraine, parts of the Holy Roman Empire and the Rhone Valley were in turn devastated by marauding gangs of brigands.

But the most important aspect of the war was the way in which its original cause changed as it progressed. It started in 1337 as a feudal quarrel between an overlord and his vassal as can be seen from terms like "seizure of fiefs", "refusal of homage" and other vocabulary from the feudal system which was used in the dispute. But by the end of the century the struggle took on a more nationalistic character and by 1420 it was definitely a war between two peoples seeking to form themselves into two modern states. With its succession of bloody massacres, plagues and pillaging, the Hundred Years War does not paint a very pretty picture of the late fourteenth and early fifteenth centuries. It is therefore hardly surprising if the people of those days, surrounded by fighting and death, often despaired of ever creating a better society.

But by the end of the fifteenth century, with economic recovery, administrative reform, the invention of the printing press and the first voyages of discovery around the globe, the era of the Hundred Years War ended with the dawning of the Renaissance.

Peasants and Nobles

Villeins, serfs, cottagers, villagers, freeholders, vassals; since the eleventh century the names for different kinds of peasants and agricultural workers increased at a steady rate. A large number of names for a large number of people: by 1300 some 90 per cent of the population of Western Europe fell into one of these categories. But very few of these workers actually owned the land that they cultivated. Most of them worked small plots which were part of a larger estate. This social structure of rural feudalism was known as the manorial system in England, and in France as the *seigneurie*. The lord could be anything from a high-ranking nobleman to a simple knight or, especially in southern France, a rich merchant or other businessman. Equally important were the ecclesiastical landowners such as abbeys, churches or cathedral chapters. The church possessions on both sides of the Channel at this time were enormous.

An average manor or estate would have covered some 150 hectares and included fields, woods, vineyards,

Land clearing for agricultural development in the years 1250-1300 was much harder than it had been in the eleventh and twelfth centuries. The best of the arable land had already been cultivated and only rough or inaccessible areas were left. Yields were poor and the ground had to be left fallow from time to time or nothing could be grown in it. A lack of good pasture meant that flocks had to graze in forests or on the fallow land. Thus, at the start of the fourteenth century, the steady rise in population and the shortage of arable land led to food shortages and undernourishment.

perhaps a village and always the residence of the overlord or his agent. This could be anything from a castle or chateau to a manor house or church. The estate was divided into two roughly equal parts. One half, the glebe land, was leased to the peasants for life in return for work or field service on the lord's own land. The other half, called demesne land, might be run by a bailiff and all the produce or revenue from it was the overlord's personal property. Usually the demesne land produced much higher yields of crops than glebe land. But the manorial system affected every aspect of the peasants' life. The lord not only had the right to collect taxes from his tenants but he also made them use his own mills, bread-ovens, wine presses and so on to process their own harvest, and claimed a proportion of the harvest in payment. He settled legal disputes amongst his tenants and imposed fines, which he kept for himself. His tenants were also required to work on the maintenance of roads and buildings, and in one case were reported to be made to beat the castle moat at night to stop croaking frogs from disturbing his sleep!

In addition to the payments and services due to their own overlord, the tenants also had to pay tithes on all harvests to the Church. Also they could be forbidden to hunt, fish or even cut down trees in the forests for themselves. But the peasantry did try to improve their lot by organising themselves into specialised economic working units. We read from the records of the estate of Great Horwood in Buckinghamshire in 1306 that collective labour was arranged to ensure the harvest was gathered in by a specific date, that all the sheep were sheared at the same time, and forestry work was done at an agreed date. But perhaps the greatest advantage that the system had for the peasants was that the lord could not increase the rents for his land and they had the absolute right to retain and inherit their tenancies "for ever". Prices had risen sharply since the early eleventh century so this really meant that the peasants' land was almost rent free.

The peasants' daily life was very hard. It was difficult for them to keep their families fed and clothed when all they had was a hectare or two of land, basic iron tools and a few animals. Lack of food meant the peasants had no defence against any disasters; bad harvests led to famine and epidemics.

From the end of the thirteenth century the rise in population forced increasingly large families to live under the one roof. The hearth was the centre of family life and the first nationwide censuses, taken in France (1328) and England (1377), for tax assessments, simply counted the number of "hearths" in the countryside.

Once or twice a year the peasants came to the overlord's manor or castle to pay their dues: a few copper coins for their land rent, chickens, geese, eggs, bread or firewood as part of their contribution to the upkeep of the manorial household. These visits were also proof to the overlord that they were still his tenants and so subject to his authority.

The Two Kingdoms

From the thirteenth century sheep-rearing and the wool trade were the backbone of the English economy. The larger flocks often numbered as many as 20,000 animals.

At the beginning of the war, England had a population of less than four million compared with the seventeen million inhabitants of France. London was the only really large city, having a population of about 40,000 compared with the 200,000 people living in Paris, which was one of the largest cities in the western world. Also the area of France, at 450,000 square kilometres, was nearly twice that of England. From these statistics it would appear that King Philip VI of France had the advantage, despite the fact that his kingdom was scattered over a large area, which became even more widespread from the twelfth century onwards. The increasingly powerful merchants, especially in Artois and Flanders, played a key role in maintaining a brisk circulation of money which kept the economy healthy. A whole range of taxes, duties and levies on revenue gave the king a permanent and stable source of income.

But the strength of the English economy must not be underestimated. The agricultural system was well

organised and more efficient than in France, and it contributed greatly to the economy. Also the government of the country had been centralised for several centuries. The respective roles and power of the king and parliament (made up of the barons, knights and upper middle classes) had been clearly defined in the preceding century. Sheriffs carried out the king's decrees in each county, while the wheels of justice and finance turned smoothly even in the smallest village.

Ireland and Wales, conquered in the twelfth and thirteenth centuries, remained hostile to the crown and, after its defeat at Bannockburn in 1314, the English army had never gained a lasting foothold in Scotland. But England still held important continental possessions, such as Bordeaux and Guyenne, which were crucial to English trade.

Furthermore, King Edward III pursued an active diplomatic policy, which gained him strong allies, such as the German Holy Roman Emperor, Ludwig IV, and several Rhineland princes. However, Philip VI could count on the support of the Duchies of Brittany and Burgundy, as well as that of the Count of Flanders, whom he supported during an uprising in 1328. The Papacy, which had been installed at Avignon, on France's south-eastern borders, since 1309, was also more likely to take the French side in any dispute.

In many respects, the two kingdoms were very similar, particularly in their way of life and their economic priorities. Both sides wanted more land. Many landowners found themselves lords of extremely small properties, as a result of the custom of dividing up estates between younger sons. One example of this was Adam de Mitry, a knight who lived just south of Paris. His estate, in 1310, consisted of a house, garden and three hectares, no more than a peasant might have. Generally the economic situation was clear: estates brought in very small revenues, the selling price of cereal crops was poor and tenants' rents were very low. On the other hand the price of goods, materials, tools and agricultural labourers' wages had risen. What was the solution? Naturally, many noblemen tried to make their peasants work harder, to extract more from them in fines through the law courts and to increase taxes... But for the thousands of small landowners, knights, and even squires, who did not have any land, the appeal of a war with its profitable booty offered an instant solution to all their problems.

The monetary system dated back to the reign of Charlemagne (from AD 800 onwards). One pound was worth 20 shillings and a shilling was worth 12 pence. There were two types of financial transactions: one dealt purely with accountancy, that is assessing incomes, taxes, etc. (calculated in pounds) while the other used the coinage in circulation (pieces of gold, silver or copper). The value of coins was assessed in several ways: the size; the percentage of precious metal to alloy in each coin; and the exchange rate. Money could be devalued by reducing the weight or size of coins, increasing the percentage of alloy in the coinage or by extending unsecured credit.

The value of money went down in wartime, for example in Flanders in 1317 the silver groat weighed 4 grams, in 1383 one gram and by 1467 just 0.7 grams. As yet no single international monetary system existed. All sorts of different coins were in circulation throughout Europe, including Byzantine and Arab money. It was from this chaotic system that the great money-changers sprang up. They made their fortunes by weighing and assessing the relative values of different coins.

The Origins of the War

It was at Amiens Cathedral on June 6, 1329, that Edward III did homage to Philip VI for the duchy of Guyenne. Placing his hands in those of Philip, the English king said that he was a "man of the king of France for the duchy of Guyenne and its lands." (Illumination from a manuscript in the Great Chronicles of France, c.1375. Bibliothèque Nationale, Paris.)

The Treaty of Paris in 1259 ended a long struggle between the kings of France (the Capets) and the kings of England (the Plantagenets). But ever since the time of Saint Louis (King Louis IX of France, 1226-70) the two houses had come into conflict in their roles as overlords and vassals. French kings were no longer prepared to put up with foreign rulers holding fiefs in France. They tried everything they could in an effort to regain the province of Aquitaine, finally asserting that its Duke, (who was the king of England), held it in fief from the French crown. And in turn the English kings were far from happy with their rather humiliating position in Aquitaine and continually looked for ways to gain more independence for their French possessions.

But the treaty of 1259 did not draw a clear boundary between the province of Aquitaine and the rest of the French kingdom. This provoked many legal disputes, and the French king and his agents capitalised on them. In October 1323, men in the service of the seneschal of the duchy of Guyenne in eastern Aquitaine, protecting the interests of the king of England, destroyed the fortified town of Saint Sardos, near Agen. The town had been built by men serving the French king, and the latter used the incident as an excuse to confiscate the whole of Guyenne, which was only returned to the English king after it had been considerably reduced in size. As well as making military intrusions into the province, the French king's men also encroached on other ducal rights, and entered the duchy without authority to carry out arrests or seize possessions.

The economic prosperity of Guyenne increased the bad feeling between the two sides. Every year hundreds of boats exported wine from Bordeaux to England. At the same time, in Flanders, the fact that the Count of Flanders was a vassal of the French king was not welcomed by the

Flemish merchants, who depended heavily on their trade with England for their livelihood. The Flemish textile industry depended on imported English wool for its raw materials, and as a result of this trade towns such as Ghent, Bruges and Ypres grew enormously in wealth and size. But the English crown also depended on the Flemish markets for a large part of its revenue. In August 1328, the French intervened on behalf of the Count of Flanders by crushing a merchants' revolt at Cassel. The French king was attempting to get the Flemish towns firmly on his side before turning his sights on London.

From 1328 a third major bone of contention was added to the feudal and economic disputes: the question of succession to the French throne. The French king, Charles IV, third son of Philip the Fair (Philip IV), died without children or surviving brothers. The barons chose, first as regent and then as king, a German prince who was a cousin of Charles, Philip of Valois. They preferred a great nobleman who was also "French born" to the other claimant, Edward III of England. Edward was a grandson of Philip the Fair, but through his mother Isabella. Nonetheless in 1329 Edward paid homage to Philip of Valois, now Philip VI of France, recognising him as his overlord in Guyenne. He hoped that by settling any disputes over the situation in Guyenne he might be left a free hand to pursue his ambitions in Scotland. For a long time the English crown had been trying to conquer its northern neighbour, but the Scots resisted stoutly, with the support of the king of France. Things came to a head in 1336 when Philip VI assembled an invasion fleet in Normandy. Edward responded by speeding up military preparations to combat any invasion. At the same time he welcomed Robert of Artois, brother-in-law of the French king, who had recently had his lands in Flanders confiscated by Philip. Robert urged Edward to take military action against France, assuring him of support from several French barons.

The situation soon escalated when, in May 1337, Philip once more annexed Guyenne. Edward then decided to act. He renounced his homage made at Amiens in 1329 and claimed to be the true heir to the French throne, a claim he maintained he had never given up. On November 1, All Saints' Day, 1337, he finally declared war on "Philip of Valois, self-styled king of France".

Using an old feudal right of appeal, the peasants put their cases before the representatives of the French king to query decisions made in the courts of the Duke of Guyenne...who was the king of England.

Knights and Fighting Men

On both sides of the Channel the main royal armies were formed by the feudal dues of service. In time of war, holders of fiefs, vassals of the king, knights and esquires were called up by order of the sovereign, who also expected them to provide an agreed number of foot-soldiers, as well as their own horses and military equipment.

The king could also call up all his subjects who were old enough to bear arms. These included men of good standing and influence from the militias that formed the defence of every town and city. In France, some militias had become so powerful in battle that they became a potential threat to the power of the monarchy. As a result, the French king preferred to ask the townsfolk, the rural communities and even the Church to support the war effort by paying subsidies of money rather than providing fighting men.

In England the attitude to recruitment was quite different. The campaigns in Wales and Scotland at the end of the thirteenth century had shown the importance of infantry, which by 1335 formed 50 per cent of Edward III's army. Its great strength lay in its archers, recruited mostly from the English and Welsh yeomanry. They were often mounted and practised regularly using the longbow, which measured between 1.65 and 1.85 metres in height and could pierce a coat of

At the start of the fourteenth century knights began to reinforce their coats of chain mail with metal plates to protect the arms, legs and hands. They also gave up the helmets called "great helms", which had become heavy and cumbersome, in favour of the smaller bassinet with eye-holes in a pointed or "pig-faced" visor. This could be lowered to protect the face when fighting.

Different types of fourteenth century infantrymen: above, an English soldier about 1330 armed with a pole-axe. Right, two foot soldiers armed with an axe and a bill hook. A soldier wearing a chain mail coat and bearing a huge pole-axe. If the weapons seemed an odd mixture they had one thing in common. They could stop a charging knight, unseat him or cut him down, and then finish him off when he was easy prey on the ground.

chain-mail at 200 metres. While a crossbow bolt was more accurate and could kill at 400 metres, its disadvantage lay in the speed of reloading: a crossbow could only be fired twice a minute but a longbow could fire 10 to 12 arrows per minute.

The feudal system limited the number of days' service due from any man in one year; its armies could not be organised to fight long campaigns. Each side therefore had to add to its forces with mercenaries. These men were recruited and commanded by a "captain" who would enter into a contract with the leader of the side the mercenaries were supporting. For example, in 1369, the English baron John Neville signed a contract to support the Duke of Lancaster with 20 armed men and 20 archers, all fully equipped, at a cost of 500 English Marks a year, and the contract included a clause which would repay him for every horse lost in battle. Usually such a contract would be drawn up in duplicate in two columns on the left and right hand sides of the same piece of parchment and then cut in two down the middle in a zig-zag line with a razor. Each party kept one half of the contract and, when it came to settling up, the two "indentures" were slotted together to prove the document was genuine.

Methods of warfare had changed little since the twelfth and thirteenth centuries and large pitched battles were rare. Fortified towns and castles played a major role in campaigns, as no advancing army could afford to leave a fully-garrisoned enemy stronghold behind it. Sieges were very common and gunpowder, introduced into Europe at the end of the twelfth century, began to play an important military role. The English used gunpowder to bombard the Scots in 1333. In all, Edward III could raise an army of about 15,000 men. In France, Philip VI had in theory a huge number of soldiers at his disposal. But shortage of money and poor communications made it difficult to assemble as many troops as he might have wanted. Indeed, the cost of assembling and maintaining a large army was so great that both kings were reluctant to go on the offensive.

Having set sail for the continent in 1337 to support the Flemish revolt, Edward actually played for time until 1339. Philip went to meet him with about 20,000 men, but could not take the risk of fighting a really decisive battle. Meantime the two armies pillaged and plundered the countryside round Cambrésis, Thiérache and the Vermandois, until finally Edward ran out of money and withdrew.

The sword was still the knights' favourite weapon in the four-teenth century. Usually wielded in one hand only, it could be supple-mented with a long, thin, very sharp dagger.

The Opening Battles

The battle of Sluys, June 24, 1340. Naval battles were rare in the Hundred Years War, but loss of life was colossal when they occurred. The fleets were made up of galleys and a new type of vessel called a "Cog". The huge, broadsided, pointed vessels were equally useful as cargo ships in peacetime. In war they could carry large numbers of horses and men at a time, together with their heavy equipment, and even cannons.

The two fleets lined up facing each other at battle stations. The French army, in 200 ships, took up a position in front of Sluys, the Channel port for the Flemish town of Bruges. At anchor in a line several kilometres wide, the English fleet, commanded by Edward III himself, barred the way to the open sea. On the morning of June 24, 1340, the French admirals decided to break through the English blockade. But the English, with the sun, wind and current behind them, advanced. Their archers, using longbows, were able to unleash a hail of murderous arrows whilst still a long distance away. The crossbows of the Genoese mercenaries on the French ships could not reply with anything like the same speed. Soon the French fleet was within range of huge boulders which the English hurled at them, the stones tearing holes in the French sails and rigging. Unable to move, the French ships were then boarded and fierce hand-to-hand fighting with axe, sword and lance followed. Thousands of men were killed, many of them by drowning.

France lost its entire fleet at Sluys in what was the first real battle of the war. From then on the English could land where and when they liked on

the French coast, but for the time being the war petered out into a series of skirmishes.

It was the death of Count Jean III of Brittany and the dispute over the succession to his Duchy that rekindled hostilities in 1341. Edward had a few minor successes in Brittany but had not so far managed to win a decisive victory. But warfare was an expensive business and Edward was soon able to see a way to replenish the royal coffers when a Norman nobleman, Geoffroy d'Harcourt, who had been banished from France, advised him to attack Normandy. Badly defended, this rich province was a tempting prize. In July, 1346, Edward crossed the Channel, landed in Normandy and laid waste the countryside, plundering the town of Caen. The English army then advanced as far as the river Seine but, in order to avoid direct combat with the huge French army on the opposite bank of the river, they veered north towards Flanders. Weighed down with their booty, worn out by forced marches and badly fed they were soon caught by the French. In order to face an army vastly superior in numbers, Edward encamped in a fortified position near the village of Crécy on August 26. Then he drew up his battle lines. The English and Welsh bowmen took cover behind hedges and carts. In front of them Philip advanced with his Genoese crossbowmen.

The French lines of foot-soldiers were soon shattered by the English arrows. Terrified, the survivors retreated in disarray. But the French knights, scornful of these cowardly soldiers, charged headlong into the fray only to be cut down by the English archers in their turn. In the appalling carnage thousands of men and horses died from suffocation, and the English cavalry and infantry then moved in to finish off both the floundering survivors and wounded. Philip himself managed to escape from the battlefield but his knights had paid very dearly for their outdated ideas of chivalry and warfare.

After such an unexpected victory, Edward was interested only in returning to his own country. He besieged Calais and, with the French king unwilling to fight another battle, the port fell on August 4, 1347. The English had now established an invaluable bridgehead on the continent, directly opposite the port of Dover.

The Ravages of the Black Death

When asked for an explanation of the cause of the Black Death, the faculty of medicine at Paris University explained that several planets had caused "a lethal pollution of the earth's atmosphere". When asked for a cure they replied that as the epidemic had been brought about by God, "we can advise nothing except total submission to God's will, and trying any medical cures that might be offered".

Through deserted streets silent, hooded figures pulled a cart piled high with coffins. Nobody watched them pass. Doors, shutters and blinds were shut fast. In the spring of 1348, Avignon had become the latest victim of the plague, one of the greatest scourges mankind has ever known. Within a few weeks the city and its suburbs had been ravaged by the deadly plague, and a new cemetery opened specially for the victims which already contained some 10,000 corpses!

Europe had not known such a disaster since the ninth century. In 1346 an epidemic of plague, originating in Asia, reached the shores of the Black Sea. The following year Genoese ships carried the terrible illness from Constantinople to ports on the western Mediterranean. From 1348 to 1352 the Black Death, so called because it turned the skin of its victims black, swept across Europe from Portugal to Russia.

An outbreak was usually detected a few weeks before it took hold. As soon as the first cases were diagnosed in a town, the people panicked. Cries of "The plague! The plague", could be heard everywhere. Church bells tolled to warn the citizens, but in fact made

the panic worse. The Church was of little comfort as it saw the scourge as a divine punishment, as foretold by the Four Horsemen of the Apocalypse, described in the Book of Revelation in the Bible. Science could offer no help either. Doctors were helpless when confronted by the epidemic. They attributed it to astrological causes, such as comets or eclipses, which they believed had poisoned the ground and the air. Only a few doctors knew about such basic precautions as boiling drinking water and burning infected corpses. But the only really safe way of combatting the plague was to flee early, quickly and as far away from it as possible.

On realising that the crowded conditions of the towns caused the disease to spread rapidly, the rich and powerful fled to the countryside. But the very poor had to stay behind. Soon cities had to shut their gates and their inhabitants were left alone to face their fate. Normal life virtually disappeared. Survivors avoided each other for fear of infection, staying indoors and leaving dead bodies outside. They hung on in the hope of surviving, but very few ever did so.

The loss of human life was quite staggering. According to Froissart, the Black Death was believed to have killed about one third of the world's population. Between 1348 and the census of 1377 the population of

England fell by 40 per cent due to "plagues". It should be remembered that by this time any epidemic, typhoid, diptheria or smallpox, was thought to be the plague.

The helpless population looked for scapegoats and blamed foreigners, lepers and in particular Jews for the epidemic. Such cries as : "Death to the Jews! They have poisoned our springs and our wells! The Jews brought the plague!" were common. Everywhere in Europe anti-semitism was widespread and broke out in violent attacks, which began in Spain and reached a peak in Germany and Alsace. Half the Jewish population of Strasbourg was burned at the stake in 1349. The Pope, however, cleared the Jews of any blame for the Black Death and insisted that only by prayer and penance could God's anger be calmed. But, horrific though it was in terms of human suffering, the Black Death did force both sides in the Hundred Years War to stop all military activity for several years.

In an attempt to soften God's anger, many of the people took part in countless penitential processions. From them the sect called "Flagellants" spread and gained vast numbers of followers throughout Europe. They were responsible for many incidents of mass hysteria.

The chronicler Jean de Venette described them in this way: "Barelegged, they travelled through public streets and the main squares of towns and villages in long processions, followed by vast crowds. They walked naked, with each man carrying a whip to lash the person in front of him. The pointed thongs cracked to the rhythm of screaming and chanting". Occasionally they turned their whips upon the local Jews. The movement was swiftly condemned by the Pope.

19

"The King Checked"

As Europe began to recover from the effects of the Black Death, local truces were broken and hostilities were resumed. Negotiations had broken down between England and the new French king, John II, known as "The Good", who succeeded Philip VI in 1350. There was no way that John could bring himself to give up his rights in Aquitaine, even if Edward were to renounce his own claims to the French throne. In the autumn of 1355, an English expeditionary force destroyed much of Languedoc as far south-east as Carcassonne, whose suburbs were pillaged and razed to the ground.

King John, like his father, held chivalrous but outdated ideas about warfare, but nevertheless he tried to learn the lessons of Crécy and to prepare his forces for the inevitable conflict. Many French soldiers were equipped with lighter, more mobile armour, and a troop of archers was specially recruited. Wages were increased and discipline tightened.

But the French crown still faced enormous problems in financing the war effort. The value of money had depreciated by 70 per cent in the first five years of John's reign, and in 1355 the king had to summon the Estates General to ask for financial help. This assembly, representing the three main orders of the country (the nobles, the Church and the wealthy middle classes) granted the necessary money but on condition that they controlled how it should be raised and how it should be spent. It was the first time in French history that the Estates General had gained any direct control over the royal finances.

The battle of Poitiers

In the summer of 1356 the Black Prince, eldest son of Edward III, led a new and daring raid into France. Setting out from Bordeaux at the head of an army of about 6 – 7,000 English and Gascon troops he headed for the Loire valley. The Limousin and the duchy of Berry were crushed and pillaged. But the approach of the main French army, commanded by King John himself, and vastly superior in numbers, forced the Black Prince to turn back. Weighed down with booty his army was soon overtaken and had to join battle between Maupertuis and Nouaillé wood, near Poitiers, on September 19.

Half-hearted attempts at negotiating a truce gave the English invaluable time to take up a strong position. The archers were dug in behind a long stretch of thick hedge. The French knights dismounted, preferring to advance and fight on foot despite their heavy armour. To cries of "Saint George" and "Saint Denis" the battle began. But almost immediately the storm of English arrows caused panic among the French knights, who had great difficulty in moving quickly. At the sight of the carnage many Frenchmen fled, including the king's eldest son Charles. But John stood his ground with his younger son Philip and a small band of soldiers, determined to fight to the death. As Froissart put it, "The French king knew full well that his people and his country

The battle of Poitiers, September 19, 1356. (Illumination from Froissart's Chronicles, late fifteenth century. Bibliothèque Nationale, Paris.)

were in peril as standards and banners were flung away all round him and his troops broke ranks and retreated before the force of their enemies". John was twice wounded but eventually he and about 2,000 of his men were over whelmed and surrendered. The cry went up, "King John has been captured!". The dreadful news spread like wildfire from the battlefield to all parts of the kingdom. Thinking that he had salvaged his country's honour, the king had in fact plunged the country into turmoil and disarray. Many nobles returned home only to be greeted with cries of "Traitors!" and "Cowards!".

The Dauphin Charles was now forced to assume the royal responsibilities. But he was only eighteen years old and could hardly be expected, with his lack of physical strength, to be up to dealing with such a dramatic change in his country's fortunes. The almost nationwide discontent was further complicated by a new pretender to the French crown, Charles, King of Navarre and Count of Evreux and Mortain in Normandy. A prince of the French royal blood, in fact he had as good a claim to the throne as either Edward III or John II.

In order to get more money the Dauphin, like his father, had to summon the Estates General. Eight hundred representatives of the three orders met on October 17, 1356, in Paris amid an atmosphere of great civil unrest. The people, afraid of a foreign invasion, wanted to strengthen the city's defences. They chose as their leader Etienne Marcel, Provost of Paris and a representative at the Estates General.

On the night of his victory at Poitiers, the Black Prince welcomed his prisoner, the king of France, in his own tent. "He ordered wine and food to be brought and served the king himself as a sign of the very great honour in which he held him," Froissart wrote in his chronicles.

Trade Routes

Fairs were the main meeting places where merchants gathered to chat and carry out deals. They lasted several weeks. The first week was devoted to setting up stalls and trading posts, then several days' trading would take place and at least ten days were needed to add up the accounts and pack goods up afterwards. In France, from 1260 onwards, the old fair sites in Champagne were replaced by new fairs held in Paris. The most famous of these was held in June at Lendit, near the Paris suburb of Saint Denis. But in the fourteenth century war and insecurity made many merchants give France a wide berth and by 1360 the few fairs that were left attracted only local traders. (Bibliothèque Nationale, Paris.)

"No king, no prince nor any other man has as high a reputation or stands in such good credit as a successful merchant." So wrote Cotrugli, a wealthy merchant from the Italian city of Ragusa, in the fifteenth century. He went on to add that only merchants could be good financiers as they alone bought, sold, delivered and traded in the goods which were needed by both the urban and rural populations.

Trade routes at this time covered the length and breadth of Europe. On the roads, traders ranged from modest pedlars to wealthy merchants with large wagon trains. The rivers and waterways were congested with barges heavily laden with cargo. Ever since the twelfth century the great commercial use of sea routes, which were faster and cheaper, had led to a revolution in ship building and navigational aids such as the compass. Cogs and smacks and other small cargo boats from Germany, larger Genoese vessels and stately Venetian merchant ships could carry anything up to 300 tonnes of merchandise. Ships brought wine from

Bordeaux and other parts of Gascony to London, where they collected English wool which was bound for Flanders. The German merchants of the Hanseatic towns shipped corn from the Baltic countries southwards to Spain and North Africa and returned with cargoes of salt from Brittany or the Vendée in France. But the most important European merchants and traders were the Italians. The Genoese went as far as the Black Sea in search of gold, furs, spices and alum – an essential commodity in dyeing textiles. The Venetians had been trading with the Arab peoples of Syria and Egypt for centuries. But all these enterprises took a long time to set up and to carry out. It could take up to two years to collect spices in Alexandria and transport them to London via Venice and then return with a cargo of tin.

The risks were great both on land and sea. At sea, shipwreck and pirate raids: on land, ambushes by brigands and robbers both resulted in the loss of ships, wagons and cargoes. This led to the forming, from 1350 onwards, of trading companies which insured their goods and vessels with Italian bankers. These companies, made up of individual merchants, undertook joint trading enterprises which were underwritten by the insuring bankers. Depending on the amount of capital invested by each merchant the bankers would share out the profits amongst them on the completion of a journey or would reimburse any losses. No merchant was stupid enough to travel with a large sum of money. Instead

Popular literature of the times often branded sea merchants as stupid and timid. But in truth, during the long weeks spent at sea, the merchants often had to take up swords to defend their lives and cargoes.

they used international drafts in the form of notes of credit from bankers and merchants in one country which would be honoured by their representatives in another. The great Florentine, Genoese and Venetian bankers had trading posts, offices or branches throughout Europe, Asia and North Africa where such notes were exchanged according to their local value. Indeed, in their role as international bankers and money changers, the great finance houses invested money from their clients – nobles, clergy and lawyers – in their own businesses.

As money lenders they perfected the art of accounting. The major companies knew at any given time the exact value of their business and could tell merchants the value of their goods. They also advanced money on credit to finance the first military campaigns of 1337 – 1346. Edward III borrowed the enormous sum of one and a half million gold florins from the Bardi and Peruzzi bankers of Florence to finance the war against France. Just how large this sum was can be appreciated when compared with the purchase by the Papacy of the entire city of Avignon for just 80,000 florins in 1348! Such a large loan proved to be a bad investment. The Bardi went bankrupt in 1343 and the Peruzzi three years later, so the English king never had to repay his creditors.

Mediaeval merchants were a strong group. Cotrugli wrote: "I have seen great men who, when ruined, were quite happy to hire out their horses to wagonners, take jobs as agents for other merchants or even become innkeepers". The sole aim of the merchant was to get rich, even though his methods might clash with the teaching of the Church, which forbade making a profit out of lending money. As their wealth increased, merchants became socially more acceptable and influential. Many became magistrates or aldermen and effectively governed their towns. The major Italian cities and all the Flemish wool towns were run by the wealthiest middle class merchants. Some merchants went on to buy noble titles for themselves or assured them for their heirs by marrying into the nobility. This sometimes resulted in a merchant being able to give up trade altogether. But the most important change was that their wealth gave them as much political as economic power in European affairs.

The main goods traded were cloth, spices, cereals, weapons, wooden and iron tools and implements. It is worth noting the large number of household goods such as earthenware jars, copper pots and pans, dishes and plates of beaten metal bought and sold at the fairs.

Etienne Marcel

On February 22, 1358, Etienne Marcel and his troops broke into the Dauphin's palace. For several months the Provost was master of Paris.

On October 16, 1356, just one month after the defeat at Poitiers, the Estates General met in the Parliament building in Paris. Amongst the deputies one voice could be heard above the rest shouting, "We must punish the Dauphin's bad advisers and reform the economy to return to the prosperous days of Saint Louis! We must raise a strong army and oust the English once and for all. We should levy taxes on everybody, the nobility and clergy included!".

The speaker was the most powerful businessman in Paris, Etienne Marcel. As the Provost of the merchants he controlled the city militia. He made himself spokesman for those rich Parisians who wanted to reform the country and, above all, control the royal finances through the Estates General.

Faced with such an eloquent and influential figure as Marcel, the inexperienced young Dauphin, Charles, tried to play for time. He suspended the session but, faced with the problem of the royal treasury, was forced to re-summon the deputies and give way to their demands. Some of his advisers were arrested, and

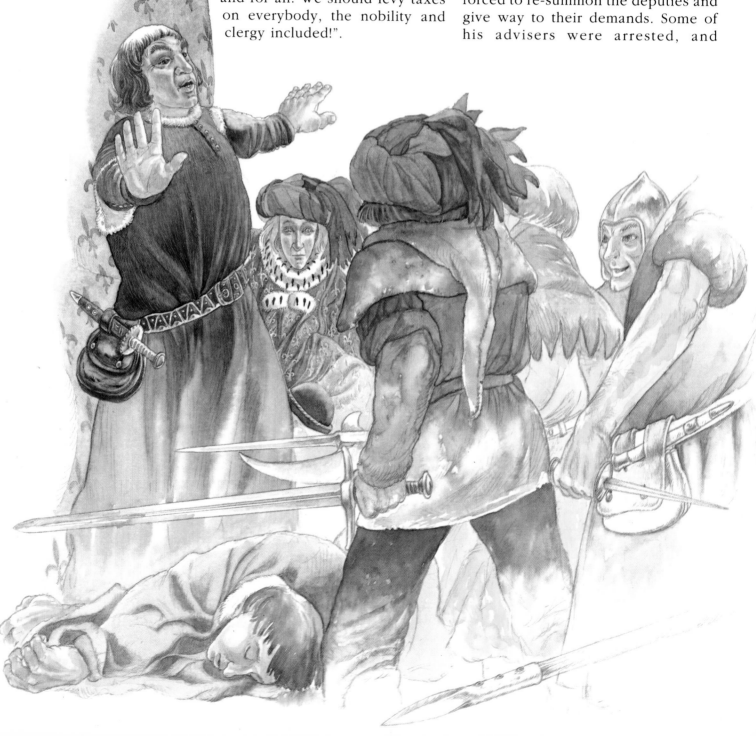

Left, men of the Paris city militia in their blue and red uniforms, the city colours, and a kind of iron helmet called a kettle hat.
Right, the assassination of the marshalls of Champagne and Normandy in 1358.
(Extract from an illuminated manuscript of the Great Chronicles of France, c.1375. Bibliothèque Nationale, Paris.)

administrative reforms were drawn up in the Great Ordinance of March 1357.

The unrest in Paris died down for a while after this success, but Charles, for all his apparent weakness, was not prepared to be dictated to in this way. In the following year Etienne Marcel decided to enforce the reforms by violence. He used the militia to invade the royal palace. On February 22 the Provost himself led his troops into the palace, where they hauled out and murdered the Marshals of Normandy and Champagne. As the finishing touch to his victory Marcel crowned the Dauphin with the blue and red helmet of the city guard. The mob then made for the town hall in the Place de Grève where Marcel addressed them from a window of the building. "The blood of these traitors has been shed for the good of the kingdom!" he shouted. "Put your trust in me."

Looking for supporters among the nobility, the Provost found an ally in Charles of Navarre, fresh from his success against the recent peasant uprisings. The Dauphin, afraid of becoming a hostage in Paris, escaped to the Champagne region where he raised a small army. He then took the title of Regent and guaranteed to safeguard national unity while his father, John II, remained a prisoner in London.

This proved to be a clever move. Support for the bullying Provost collapsed, as the wealthier citizens saw no future in the economic chaos that now reigned in the capital, and the nobles disliked the proposed military and economic reforms. As the Dauphin's troops approached Paris, Etienne Marcel tried to bring his supporters, the Navarrese and English troops, into the city. On July 31, 1358, he tried to open the Saint Antoine gate to his allies. The Paris mob, realising what he was doing and infuriated by such treachery, set upon him and hacked him to death on the pavement. The Dauphin was now able to re-enter the capital, where he revoked all the concessions that he had been forced to make to the Provost. The Paris uprising had failed.

Seal of the Hanseatic maritime merchants of the port of Paris (thirteenth century).

A World in Turmoil

Only a few major ports of western Europe, such as Genoa, Bruges, London and Bordeaux, were equipped with large cranes which allowed heavy cargoes to be unloaded on the quayside.

In these very dangerous times most towns and cities were protected by high towers, fortified walls and drawbridges. Paris and London had been fortified for a long time, but towns such as Louvain, Brussels and Strasbourg now also had to protect themselves. Many had only hastily erected and incomplete defences. Whether they were the property or seat of a bishop, a city with a royal charter, or a large port or trading centre, the towns of the fourteenth and fifteenth centuries were the centre of constant commercial activity: fairs, craft centres, heavy industry and above all banking and money-changing.

With the countryside becoming less safe, in an age of roving bands of robbers and pillagers, each town attracted immigrants from the surrounding regions. This led to suburbs springing up outside the city walls, around the fortifications, at gates, busy crossroads or close to main roads and waterways serving the town. These suburbs soon became important trading places themselves which merchants could abandon in times of trouble to seek shelter within the city walls.

Apart from completely new towns which were built in the twelfth and thirteenth centuries, mediaeval towns were seldom built to a set plan. The architecture and street planning were haphazard. The lanes, narrow and

twisting, often ended in blind alleys or the courtyards of buildings. Some cities, such as Bruges and Ghent on tributaries of the Lys and the Escaut, sprawled along the banks of busy rivers.

Cathedrals, churches, belfries, fortified houses of the nobility and the sumptuous residences of the wealthiest merchants overshadowed the ordinary town buildings. In Northern Europe most houses had only two floors and within the city walls there were large areas of open land. Gardens, open parkland, fields of sheep and even farms attached to abbeys were not uncommon. On the Mediterranean coasts, however, land was much more scarce and five-storey, closely packed buildings were common. One traveller on arriving in Genoa is said to have exclaimed, "The houses here are more like towers!". It was true that in this metropolis of 200,000 people, as big as Paris and five times the size of London, the density of population was the highest in Western Europe. It was estimated that in some streets Genoa housed 2,000 people to the hectare.

Even though the mediaeval town was the centre of wealth there were no separate quarters for the rich and poor. The wealthier people lived on the first floors of the buildings, the very poorest had lodgings in attics under the roofs, and at street level were the shops, booths and workshops. The noise was constant from dawn till dusk. The cooper's mallet, the carpenter's hammer, the smith's forge and the clicking of the looms resounded constantly, interspersed with the cries from animals awaiting slaughter at the butcher's.

It was usual to find one area, or even one particular street, in the town given over to just one craft or business. These would be given such names as "Tanner Street", "Oil Press Row", "Bankers' Square" etc. In the suburbs, along the riversides or the canals, industries like milling, dyeing and dressing of skins could be found. This very heavy, smelly, dirty work was done by the unskilled labourers, who were paid a pittance. They were not allowed to form their own trade associations as the more powerful guilds did not permit it. With the scum of society and the beggars they formed the lowest class of all which was often ready to break out into revolt at the least excuse. The close-knit trade, craft and merchant guilds held a monopoly on all aspects of commerce and were always able to put down any unrest amongst the workers, such as at Ghent in 1350 or Florence in 1378. In the cloth towns of Flanders and textile towns of Italy the merchants were literally all-powerful. They controlled the money, the raw materials, factories and trading outlets. The master craftsmen and merchants in the guilds were virtually salaried company directors. The guilds also held all local political power, as only their members became the city burgesses, aldermen and mayors.

In the face of such privileged groups why were the towns so attractive to ordinary people? The towns, because of their wealth, were the bustling centres of everyday life, providing entertainment with plays and colourful pageants. But, above all, they held out the opportunity of employment and a relatively safe haven. In times of crisis, when freebooters, robbers and soldiers were ravaging the countryside, the only safe place was inside the city walls.

Workers, apprentices and master-craftsmen were members of guilds which controlled their salaries and working conditions. These corporations held a monopoly on industrial production and commerce in the towns (and sometimes the countryside). They controlled production and prices of raw and finished materials so strictly that competition was impossible.

Strongly hierarchical, in theory the craft guilds allowed any artisan to rise to the status of a master by producing a "masterwork", usually a miniature model of a piece of work (the illustration shows the "masterwork" of an armourer). But in reality the majority of craftsmen who reached this status were the sons of guild masters who kept the masterships in their own families.

Marauders and Skinners

A village being pillaged by mercenaries about 1370.

Military operations continued after 1356 with the Black Prince leading raiding parties in France for four years. Then in 1360, France and England met at Brétigny, near Chartres, to draw up a peace treaty. This was finally signed at Calais.

The terms were disasterous for France. Edward was left in possession of about one-third of the kingdom (all of Aquitaine, the Limousin, Poitou, Ponthieu and Calais). This, together with a large sum of money, was the price France had to pay to ransom King John.

But the treaty brought no peace to the countryside. Having no use for mercenary troops in peacetime, the rulers paid them off, effectively depriving them of their livelihoods. But the companies of mercenaries remained united and loyal to their captains, becoming "Free Companies", or bands of roving brigands. Younger sons of impoverished noble families, peasants ruined by the war; they came in all nationalities – English, Spanish, German, Italian and French. Usually no more than a few hundred strong, these bands of marauders were nevertheless organised like regular soldiers. They obeyed the orders of their captains. They financed themselves with profits from their booty. They even had their own craftsmen, stable hands, farriers, armourers, quartermasters and tanners. Clerks went with them as accountants and almoners.

These Companies ravaged the countryside and pillaged the smaller towns. Peasants were tortured for their few belongings, road blocks set up and merchants' wagon trains ransacked for mules, cloth, skins and spices. Even abbeys were plundered. They scourged the whole of Europe including Alsace, the states of the Empire, Austria, but especially France. The worst affected regions were Burgundy, Languedoc and the Massif Central, where the hilly countryside offered them an easy refuge and hiding places to set up their headquarters. Some of the brigand captains lived like lords. One of them, Aimerigot Marchès, led a reign of terror throughout Auvergne and the Limousin in central France. He lived in a chateau, exacted large sums from his neighbours in exchange for leaving them in peace, and hired out his men to both the English and French rulers, depending on who could pay the most. Just before he died in 1391 Marchès told Froissart, "We lived and were treated like kings. When we set out on a raid the countryside trembled before us. It was a great life".

The defenceless population tried to organise themselves to combat the companies by buying them off. But they always returned a few months later. Despite using both threats and promises the central government could not control the marauders. Eventually Charles V and his counsellors thought up a solution. The king hired the Free Companies himself and sent them off to fight as far away from France as possible. In 1365 Du Guesclin was put in charge of an army of these mercenaries and took them to Spain to fight King Pedro of Castile. But throughout the fourteenth and fifteenth centuries frequent outbreaks of plague forced them, from time to time, to return to France. They scoured the countryside in desperate bands such as the "Scavengers", following up raids by other brigands and looting any left-overs. From 1430, groups called the "Skinners" tortured their victims for anything they could get out of them.

All these horrors were added to the ravages of more conventional warfare and practically ruined the French countryside.

In the fifteenth century most infantrymen wore a brigandine, or thick leather waistcoat. It was sleeveless and had a lining of fine steel straps secured by rivets, whose heads formed a pattern on the front of the jerkin. It was topped by a gorget and beaver, armour to protect the throat and lower part of the face. A kettle hat, an iron helmet with a wide brim, completed their armour.
(Musée de l'Armée, Paris.)

29

The Black Prince

The tomb of Edward of Woodstock, Prince of Wales, known as the Black Prince (1330-1376) in the chapel of The Holy Trinity in Canterbury Cathedral. His coat of arms, his armour, helmet and gauntlets, are displayed nearby.

"At this time the Lord Edward, Prince of Wales and of Aquitaine, passed away. He was the epitome of chivalry, most gifted in feats of arms and accomplished many great and noble deeds." Perhaps no event in the 50 years of Edward III's reign so touched the hearts of the people as the news of the death, in 1376, of his son, the Black Prince.

Born in 1330, at the royal manor of Woodstock near Oxford, Edward was the king's eldest son and heir to the throne. From his childhood he had been schooled in the arts of war and the manners of chivalry, with only a little academic learning. He spent long hours on horseback practising the use of the lance and the sword, as well as learning the art of hunting. What scholarly learning he received was probably a basic knowledge of the Greek philosophers, some arithmetic and a little theology.

The young warrior

The young prince fought in his first campaign at the age of 16, showing great military skill and courage at Caen and Crécy. On returning to England he ruled his county of Chester, until, in 1355, his father appointed him to the difficult post of Commander of Gascony, putting him in charge of all the English possessions in France. He became renowned for his generalship and knowledge of military tactics. The following year, when the prince destroyed the French army at Poitiers with a force less than a third the size of his enemy's, and took the French king prisoner, his fame became legendary throughout Europe.

Soon afterwards Edward III made his son Prince of Aquitaine, which had been greatly enlarged by the treaty of Brétigny. It was an extremely wealthy province and provided England with a cheap source of luxury goods, especially wine from the Bordeaux region and the rest of Gascony. The Black Prince and his wife, Joan of Kent, held the most extravagant and splendid courts at Bordeaux and Angoulême, with a succession of tournaments and feasts. The prince was also famed for his generosity. He gave valuable gifts to his friends and vassals as well as giving enormous donations to the Church. Although he played the role of the great and chivalrous prince, like so many great nobles of the age, when it came to warfare he was violent and merciless. He looked on pillaging and massacres as a normal part of successful warfare, sparing neither women nor children. His raids and campaigns throughout

Armagnac, the border areas around Toulouse, and especially the sacking of Limoges, left peasants and nobles alike afraid of the "Black Prince": perhaps so called because of his black armour but more probably because of the fear he aroused in them.

Confident of victory, he set out in 1366 to restore King Pedro to the throne of Castile, which had been usurped by Henry of Trastamara who had the support of France. The campaign started well in 1367, with victory over a force commanded by Du Guesclin at Najera. But King Pedro did not keep his promise to pay Edward and the prince returned to Aquitaine with an unpaid army. To meet this cost and to maintain his princely lifestyle he subjected the whole region to crippling taxes and soon lost any popularity he had had there.

The tide turns

The French aristocracy soon began to resent the excessive demands of the Black Prince, and appealed to the French king to help them. Like his predecessors, Charles V knew how to play on his position as a feudal overlord and summoned the prince, as his vassal, to Paris to explain. Edward replied, "We will come, but with an army of 60,000 men!" This was where he made his mistake, for one by one his subjects in Aquitaine deserted him and gave over their territories to the protection of the French king.

The Black Prince was in failing health and by 1370 could no longer ride a horse. He returned to England in 1371, unable to rise from his bed. Knowing that he would never become king he spent the rest of his life settling his debts and performing charitable works.

At his death Froissart wrote, "He had a strong faith in God and repented of all his sins more sincerely than any great prince before him".

Chivalry: truth and myth

The highest ideals of chivalry were still of the utmost importance to the nobility of the fourteenth and fifteenth centuries: defending the rights of the Church, honouring one's word, protecting the weak and respecting women. The knight's life centred round hunting, tournaments and, above all, warfare. "There's nothing like a good war!" exclaimed Jean de Bueil, for it represented the best chance to achieve honour and glory. An example of the importance attached to such valour was a tournament arranged in 1351 between 30 Breton knights and 30 French knights who swore to fight until they dropped, "so that our exploits will be sung and talked of for years to come in palace halls and great homes, at public gathering and in taverns throughout the world".

But such displays of chivalry had little place in the realities of warfare. Great battles such as Crécy, Poitiers, Agincourt and Verneuil were won by the English archers. In most cases warfare was reduced to undisciplined skirmishes and long sieges with little glory on either side. In 1373 misguided chivalry left knights frozen to death in the saddle in the Auvergne mountains. Yet cowardice and appalling cruelty abounded on the battlefield as soldiers were indiscriminately massacred if they were not worth ransoming. Profit ruled as much as honour. It was a common occurrence, if the price was right, for soldiers to change sides in the middle of a battle. In the fifteenth century technological advances produced more sophisticated weapons, and with these the age of chivalry in battle died.

In 1367 when the Black Prince won the battle of Najera, south of Pamplona, defeating the army of Henry of Trastamara and taking Du Guesclin prisoner, Pedro of Castile seemed assured of the throne in this Spanish kingdom. But the Castilian revolt and the victory of Du Guesclin in 1369 at Montiel reversed the situation. For, soon after this battle, Henry of Trastamara had Pedro executed, thus ending the English hopes of a lasting alliance with Spain.
(Extracted from an illuminated manuscript in the Great Chronicles of France, c.1375, Bibliothèque Nationale, Paris.)

Du Guesclin

The coat of arms of the Du Guesclin family.

Bertrand Du Guesclin was above all a great warrior. From boyhood he had been trained in the use of arms, and soldiering was his only career.

In May 1364, one month after the death of King John II, the French at last had a success on the battlefield. The royal troops beat an Anglo-Navarrese force, led by the Gascon Lord de Buch, at Cocherel near Vernon (between Normandy and Paris). Although in the military sense this was a minor victory, the battle was of considerable long-term significance. Firstly it put paid to Charles of Navarre's ambitions to march on Paris. As lord of a large part of Normandy and an ally of Edward III, the threat he had posed to the French throne was now greatly diminished. It allowed the new king, Charles V, recently crowned at Rheims, to start his reign on a note of optimism. Sickly, and unfit for strenuous, warlike activity, the new king was not a great military leader. But his experience as regent had made him a shrewd judge of character who knew how to choose useful men to serve him.

One of his most trusted commanders was Bertrand Du Guesclin, who had led the French army to victory at Cocherel. The eldest son of a minor Breton noble, he had found royal favour even though "he could not read, write or calculate". His military exploits in his native Britanny had established his reputation as a valiant leader of men, if not as a brilliant strategist. He had the backing of several influential nobles, amongst them the Duke of Orléans and Charles of Blois, pretender to the Duchy of Britanny, who obtained

32

many minor titles and fiefs for him and eventually the valuable earldom of Longueville. He was taken prisoner several times and the size of his ransoms, totalling over 460 kilos of gold, shows how highly he was valued as a soldier.

The military failures of the nobility and Charles V's mistrust of his arrogant and ambitious feudal vassals help to explain the meteoric rise to power of such a relatively low-born knight as Du Guesclin.

Even after he had made his fortune, Du Guesclin still remained a soldier at heart. In 1365 Charles V chose Du Guesclin to form the mercenary army of the "Free Companies" and lead them out of France and into northern Spain where the main fighting in the Anglo-French conflict was taking place. Returning from Spain, the Companies pillaged and laid waste much of Provence and gained a reputation for the worst types of butchery and looting. But, despite this, Charles kept Du Guesclin as his right-hand man as he wanted to renew direct hostilities with England. In October 1370, he gave Du Guesclin the sword and title of "Constable of France". It was a clever move for it gave France a heroic warrior who could stand up to the Black Prince.

Charles' aim was to recover the territories granted to Edward III in 1360, and to achieve this he needed to reform his army. He raised the money for this by levying new taxes and by stabilising the economy. Then, during the few years of relative peace, he recruited smaller but much better disciplined and trained Companies. Fortresses were built or repaired, and a new fleet was built and assembled near Rouen. Alliances with Castile, Scotland and Flanders further strengthened Charles' hand on the diplomatic as well as the military front. Charles also used his shrewdness and cunning to try to find an excuse for renewing hostilities with England. Under the pretext of homage due to him as an overlord, he summoned the Black Prince, as Duke of Aquitaine and Guyenne, to explain himself before the French parliament. The Prince's

threat that he would only do so with 60,000 men behind him led to a renewal of the war in the south-west and north of France. During the next ten years,

Du Guesclin receiving the sword of Constable of France from Charles V on October 2, 1370, at the Saint-Pol palace in Paris.
(Miniature by Jean Fouquet illustrating one of the manuscripts of the Great Chronicles of France, c.1475; Bibliothèque Nationale, Paris.)

The sword of the Constable of France, probably fifteenth century. The heel of the blade and the hilt were engraved with fleur-de-lis pointing towards the blade. The sword was purely a symbol of royal command and was not used for fighting. It was always carried with "the blade bare and upright".
(Musée de l'Armée, Paris.)

Du Guesclin pursued the new royal strategy of avoiding pitched battles, of which France had only bitter memories, and concentrating on brief skirmishes and sieges. This allowed the English to raid and pillage where they chose without gaining or retaining land but losing whatever popular support they may have had. As Charles V reckoned, "Better a countryside laid waste than land lost to the enemy".

This policy caused great hardship but by 1380 it had worked so well that the regions of France controlled by the English had been reduced to the area around Bordeaux and Bayonne and the port of Calais.

On July 13, 1380, Du Guesclin died of fever while besieging the fortress of Chateauneuf-de-Randon in Auvergne. As a mark of high honour, Charles allowed the commander's body to be buried in the royal vault at Saint Denis. Two months later the king followed his most famous warrior to the grave.

Chroniclers of the War

From the very beginning of the war people were fully aware of the importance of events, of the fierce battles and of the widespread changes in life brought about by the conflict. Some of them decided to record these stirring times in chronicles, describing events as they happened.

One cannot blame these chroniclers for lack of criticism and sometimes taking sides. They were writing about events as they occurred. They were not historians with the benefit of hindsight, and above all they were influenced by contemporary ideas of right and wrong. They worked hard to search out the truth, and with their inquisitive minds and the methods of communication they developed they were effectively both the reporters and diplomatic correspondents of the Hundred Years War.

As most of the fighting took place on the continent it is not surprising that the majority of chroniclers lived in or came from the areas where the conflict took place. Most of them were from the wealthy classes, and were well educated. Amongst them were noblemen such as Enguerrand de Monstrelet from Picardy (died 1453), who fought on the Burgundian side, Georges Chastellain (1405-1475) also a Burgundian supporter, and Philippe de Commynes (1447-1511) who served first Charles the Bold of Burgundy and then Louis XI of France.

Many others were clerics, notably Jehan Le Bel (died 1370) a canon of Liège, Andrew Wyntoun, a Scottish priest who was a canon in Paris and died in 1420, and Jean de Venette (died 1369) the prior of a monastery in Paris. The most famous of all of them was Jean Froissart (1333-1405) the son of a manuscript illuminator at Chimay and himself a priest at Estinnes in Brabant. Froissart, like Chastellain, was also a poet. Others such as Monstrelet and Commynes were sent on diplomatic missions. But they all had

In 1388 Froissart travelled through Bearn, ruled by Gaston Phébus, Count of Foix. In Orthez, at The Moon Inn, he met two famous Gascon mercenary leaders, Bascot de Mauléon and his cousin Captain Ernauton.

They sat around the fire and talked about the use and development of weapons. Bascot enjoyed nothing better than "to reminisce about his life as a soldier, its ups and downs, his gains and losses".

the same thing in common, a determination to record the events of their age as objectively and thoroughly as they could. In the introduction to his chronicles of the reign of Louis XI Commynes writes, "I have decided to record only what I know to be true, events which I witnessed myself or which were witnessed by men I know to be honest".

As written accounts, archive material and documents were rare, the only way to record events in those times was to mix with the people directly involved in them. Commynes and Chastellain lived in the courts of Burgundy and France where they mixed as equals with the decision-making aristocracy. Froissart travelled regularly to England, Scotland, Gascony, Italy and The Netherlands. He made long stays at the courts of Edward III and Richard II, and talked to ministers, merchants, leading churchmen and people from many walks of life. Froissart actually used the technique of interviewing people with a view to fitting their replies into the appropriate sections of his chronicles.

In the fifteenth century, Monstrelet included extracts from official documents in his narratives as well as royal letters and orders, treaties between towns and even legal writs. Fascinating as these accounts are in most cases the history is incomplete, as the authors dealt only with the material or the events which they thought were worth recording. As Jehan Le Bel admitted, he wrote only of "the great deeds and adventures of the nobility, the great feats of arms and chivalry". This was not altogether surprising as chroniclers lived with and depended upon the nobility for their protection. As most chroniclers were brought up in the ideals of chivalry their records were mainly about raids, pitched battles, extravagant feasts and tournaments. The ordinary people were often relegated to a very minor role in the narratives. Froissart does refer to the "poor people of Calais" during the siege of 1346, but ignores the appalling suffering of the peasants in the raids of mercenaries.

Only Jean de Venette touched upon the misery that war inflicted on the common people.

No chronicler tried to understand the causes of the peasants' revolts. Indeed, they all refer to them in terms such as "evil men" or "wild dogs". Overall they appeared uninterested in the economic revolution of their times, seldom referring to the political and financial power of the middle classes. In general the historical analysis in most chronicles was very basic. War was caused by kings and their counsellors. Feudal duty combined with chivalry decided the conduct and outcome of the conflict. Only Commynes, towards the end of the fifteenth century, concentrated on discussing political reform and the problems facing the king and his council.

A page from a manuscript of Froissart's Chronicle; fifteenth century copy.
(Bibliothèque Nationale, Paris.)

35

The Peasants' Revolt

In 1358 a violent peasants' revolt broke out in the countryside around Paris. This "Jacquerie", caused by economic and political repression, stretched from Normandy and Artois to Burgundy. The rebels reached Meaux, where members of the royal family were staying. But for once the French King and the Navarrese forgot their differences and massacred the peasants on June 9, 1358. (From an illuminated manuscript of Froissart's Chronicles, fifteenth century edition, Bibiothèque Nationale, Paris.)

"Things cannot continue as they are in England. As long as there are nobles and peasants, and wealth is kept in the hands of a few, men will never be equal. We all come from the same mother and father, Adam and Eve".

Gathered in churchyards after Mass, peasants listened to this message, preached from village to village by the priest John Ball. Some nodded in silent agreement, others murmured assent and still more called for action. In England, towards the end of the fourteenth century, violent unrest was beginning to turn men against their lords. The manorial system was starting to fall apart. The economic depression, caused by war and the Black Death, had greatly reduced man power and raised agricultural wages. Faced with this problem the nobility started to reassert old feudal rights by making their tenants work even harder on demesne land, a custom that had almost fallen into disuse. But above all they wanted parliament to strengthen the Statute of Labourers, a law which already limited agricultural wages and forced the peasants to continue living on the lord's land. The nobility, in short, wanted to continue the system under which all workers, freemen and bondmen, serfs and villeins were tied to their landlord for life.

The government, under the young King Richard II, was unable to stop the angry explosion of public feeling. The economic situation was disasterous, the costly war having brought in no revenue from booty for nearly 20 years. Now, in 1380, a new campaign in France had to be financed, as well as an expedition to support the king of Portugal. Added to these was the cost of the proposed marriage of Richard to the daughter of the king of Bohemia. To achieve all this the crown imposed even more crippling taxes which only aggravated the social unrest.

Their revolt was aimed against the nobility and the royal administration, and the peasants sought the abolition of the hated Statute of Labourers and of all types of forced labour. Local unrest turned to national revolt in May 1381. Rebel bands from Essex and Kent, poorly armed but well led by an ex-soldier, Wat Tyler and the clergyman, John Ball, attacked rich abbeys and even castles. These were pillaged and burnt, and the hated charters binding men to their overlords were destroyed. In this way many people obtained by force the freedoms that they were denied by law. Crown officials were killed and soon the revolt spread to London.

To shouts of "Come on, let's find the king. He's young and will listen to our grievances", tens of thousands of peasants marched on the capital. Many

artisans and other working-class Londoners sympathised with the agricultural workers and opened the gates to them on June 14. They soon overran the city, burning houses of the wealthier merchants and beating up those who were said to have exploited their workforce. The few hundred men guarding the Tower of London could not prevent it being seized and several unpopular royal advisors were killed. Although he was only 14 years old, Richard II bravely faced the mob. He tried to calm them but finally agreed to their demands by promising to abolish serfdom, repeal the Statute of Labourers, and give the peasantry a greater share of the wealth of the Church. Gloating over their success, Wat Tyler's troops gradually dispersed.

But the next day, having reinforced his troops, the king regained control of the situation. "Villeins you are and villeins you remain", he is said to have told to a group of rebel representatives who came to talk to him. Tyler and Ball were killed and the old order was brutally restored. All the promised concessions were cancelled and the revolt collapsed.

Wat Tyler's revolt was, however, of considerable importance. It had lit the flame of social unrest and the old feudal system in England never recovered. Throughout the fifteenth century other rural revolts broke out all over Europe. In the Catalonia region of Spain, Scandinavia and England peasants continued to vent their feelings of anger and despair in violent outbursts of rebellion, but without any immediate success.

In France, as in England, peasant uprisings often involved the destruction of their overlord's records. Even if they could not read, the peasants knew the importance of the documents which listed the overlord's tenants and debtors.

A Period of Truce

In September 1396 the treaty signed at Calais, between the kings of England and France, was also sealed by the marriage of Richard II to Charles VI's daughter, Isabelle. The two events were celebrated with lavish feasting. (From an illuminated manuscript of Froissart's Chronicles, fifteenth century. Bibliothèque Nationale, Paris.)

After the war had dragged on for more than fifty years both sides were in need of a respite. Heavy taxes had been levied in many countries and had led to protests and revolts: in England in 1381, and at Rouen and Paris in 1382. In Flanders, Ghent was the centre of insurrection, and here the rebels called on their English allies for support. The French then intervened and crushed the Flemish militia at Roosebeke in 1382. This state of affairs could not continue and in 1388 a truce was signed and renewed annually until 1395, when a more lasting settlement was reached between France and Flanders. This lasted for nearly 30 years until the Autumn of 1423.

Thus between 1390 and 1410, far greater security, if not actual peace, returned to most of France. As a result towns started to cut their defence budgets, and the militias were seldom called up. The English abandoned Cherbourg in 1394 and Brest three years later. Little by little commerce started to pick up, with English merchants once more trading in Rouen, and Norman merchants could be found in London and Southampton. Portuguese and Spanish traders appeared again in Honfleur, Brest, La Rochelle and Bordeaux. The money markets became more active and many Italian bankers or money changers made their fortunes out of the increase in trade.

Even so the truce was a fragile one because it had been made by the two kings alone. One of Charles VI's advisors, Robert the Hermit, was optimistic. "When the time is ripe and both kings want peace all their subjects will willingly obey them," he said.

Froissart, however, did not see the English obeying their monarch. As he observed, "the ordinary people, archers and other soldiers certainly seem more inclined to resume the war between France and England. So too do about two-thirds of the younger nobility, knights and squires who do not know what else to do with themselves". On the French side feelings were split between a desire for peace and a deep-seated hatred of the English. Charles VI was only a boy when he became king in 1380, and France had effectively been ruled by his uncles, the Dukes of Burgundy, Berry and Anjou. But in 1388 Charles, who had now come of age, removed his uncles from office and replaced them with clerics, bureaucrats and others more interested in preserving the peace.

The young king preferred to turn his attention towards the problems of the Church in Italy, trying to end the ten-year-old schism which had started after the return of the Papacy to Rome from Avignon. Following a mental breakdown in 1392, his health never again permitted him to act effectively in any capacity. The government started to crumble and the king's uncles once more took up the reins of power. Unfortunately, the Duke of Burgundy was more interested in the problems of Flanders and the Holy Roman Empire, whilst the Duke of Anjou became involved in the affairs of southern Italy. The king's brother Louis, the future Duke of Orléans, was absorbed in following up his wife's claims to the Duchy of Milan. To make matters worse, despite continual negotiations, there was no real peace. In 1393 France suggested that a province of Greater Aquitaine should be created and held as a fief from the king of France. It would be administered by John of Gaunt, the Duke of Lancaster, who was Richard II's uncle. But as the English already owned Aquitaine, by the treaty of Brétigny, their negotiators refused. They knew that any land held in fief could quite easily be repossessed by the French crown on the smallest

excuse. No other solution, acceptable to both sides, could be found.

Across the Channel Richard's autocratic attitude towards parliament and the barons turned both against him. In 1397 he made the mistake of banishing his cousin Henry Bolingbroke who was close in line to the succession through his father John of Gaunt. With public opinion behind him, Henry returned to England in 1399 as Duke of Lancaster on his father's death. He dethroned Richard and became Henry IV. This caused great concern in Paris, as Henry was known to be a strong supporter of war with France. But he continued to renew the truces until such time as England was prepared financially and militarily to resume hostilities.

On December 18, 1399, in Bruges, a merchant, Riccardo d'Alberti, deposited with the banker Guglielmo Barberi the sum of 900 Flemish crowns. The banker then signed a credit and exchange note which read: "In the name of God, the 18th day of December 1399. On presentation of this letter you are to pay the sum of 472 Barcelona pounds, worth 900 Flemish crowns, which has been deposited with me here in Bruges by Riccardo d'Alberti. May God protect you. Given at Bruges: Guglielmo Barberi" Several copies of the letter were sent to a third party, Bruniacio di Guido. He in turn presented the letter to the Barcelona office of the Datini bank which paid him the 472 pounds in local money. In this way a letter of credit was used to allow merchants to trade in different currencies and at the same time settle their bills without sending any actual cash.

Armagnacs and Burgundians

While Charles VI remained incapable of governing the country relations between his two main counsellors John the Fearless, Duke of Burgundy, and his cousin Louis of Orléans deteriorated. John was preoccupied with protecting Anglo-Flemish trade and was all for promoting peace. Louis, however, believed that it was possible to reconquer Aquitaine and started to reinforce his castles in Picardy. Nobody had enough influence or power to reconcile the two men and the situation was only resolved when, on November 23, 1407, Louis was assassinated in Paris. After the Provost's enquiry had found the Duke of Burgundy responsible for the assassination, John retired to his own Duchy to muster his troops. The new young Duke of Orléans, Charles, drew his main support from the Gascon troops of his father-in-law Bernard of Armagnac, after whom the Orléanist party took its name in the ensuing conflict.

John was a shrewd politician and he quickly sought to justify his action. The Parisians were ready to support him as he had previously rid them of the extortionate taxes and other expenses imposed on them by Louis. The University of Paris even condoned the murder, decreeing that "when a prince becomes a tyrant it is justifiable

to kill him". John promised administrative reforms and entered the city in triumph in 1413. He summoned the Estates of the "langue d'oïl" – representing the northern two-thirds of France – in order to work out these reforms. At the same time civil unrest broke out again in the capital. Burgundian supporters, the butchers' militia, under their leader Simon Caboche, hunted down and killed many Armagnacs, royal ministers and influential members of the middle classes.

The reforms drawn up in May 1413 were known as the Cabochien Ordinances because of the riots. Though they drafted many economic reforms, the appalling behaviour of the butchers so horrified the Parisians that, in August 1413, John once more decided to leave Paris. A few days later Armagnac troops moved into the city. They executed and imprisoned any Burgundians or suspected Burgundian sympathisers they could find.

This civil war between the Burgundians and Armagnacs was not just a succession of violent clashes. Financially it imposed enormous burdens on each side. Over a period of about twelve years each party appointed its own officials and counsellors, lawyers and judges to the royal court and parliament. This huge increase in the number of salaried officals, none of whom could be sure they would have a job for very long, led to the mis-use of funds in every government department. Everyone wanted to get rich while they had the chance and very soon stable government gave way to almost total anarchy.

Furthermore, from 1411 onwards, each side tried to enlist foreign support and they turned to London. In that year the Burgundians asked Henry IV for help and received 2,000 soldiers. The following year the Armagnacs promised the English king the restoration of some of his lost provinces in exchange for a contingent of 4,000 men. Then each side accused the other of treason, and the row continued into

John the Fearless, Duke of Burgundy, got his nickname in 1396 at the battle of Nicopolis against the Turks. Ever since 1361 the rich area of Burgundy had belonged to the French royal estates. It had been created a Duchy for John the Good's third son, Philip the Bold, father of John the Fearless. It soon expanded to include parts of Flanders, Artois, and the lands of the Counts of Nevers and Charolais. Taking advantage of the weak monarchy, John turned the duchy into an independent state with its own economic and bureaucratic administration.

the reign of the next English king, Henry V, who succeeded in 1413. The new king was young, ambitious and knew how to profit from the chaos in France. Henry soon demanded higher prices for his help, including the restoration of all the old Plantagenet empire as well as Flanders, Artois and Provence. Appalled by these excessively high demands, the Duke of Burgundy broke off negotiations with England. However, the Armagnacs were worried in case the English should resume the war, and persisted with their negotiations. The last French delegation arrived in England in July 1415 only to meet with a rebuff. Henry received the ambassadors and arrogantly ordered them home, adding, "I shall be right behind you!"

Civil war in Paris. In 1413 the Butchers' Company formed the majority of the city militia, which terrorised the capital in the name of the Duke of Burgundy: "one and a half to two thousand armed men wearing coats of mail, jerkins and sallets".

Agincourt

"Suddenly the sky was darkened with a cloud of arrows, glittering like rain in the sky before pouring down upon the hapless enemy", wrote Thomas of Eltham about the start of the battle. The French cavalry could not move, for "they were so closely bunched they could not even lift their swords". Maddened by the rain of arrows and the confusion, the horses unseated their riders. Meanwhile reinforcements charged up from the rear and added to the chaos by riding down their own men or getting bogged down in the mire of corpses. Their heavy armour brought them tumbling down onto their own men. Once again the English archers had got the better of the French cavalry.

During the two years of negotiations with France, Henry V, with the nation firmly supporting him, was in fact preparing for war. In the spring of 1415 he started to assemble provisions, arms and men. On August 11, the English royal fleet set sail with about 10,000 men. They landed at the mouth of the Seine a few days later and laid siege to the town of Harfleur. In face of the English cannon, which blew holes in the city walls and demolished buildings, the town surrendered within a month. But it was already too late for Henry to consider conquering the whole of Normandy that year and he decided to winter at Calais which he tried to reach via Caux and Picardy.

French reaction was slow. Both the Armagnacs and Burgundians hesitated to intervene, fearing that it would leave the other one free to take advantage of the situation. Finally the Armagnac army set out from Rouen to intercept the English. They caught up with them, on October 24, just south of Saint Omer. The English troops numbered only 6,000. They had been badly affected by an outbreak of dysentery during the siege of Harfleur and a garrison had been left behind there. These 6,000 men Henry drew up in a single line of battle, alternating archers with infantrymen. The French army of some 20,000 – 30,000 thousand cavalry and infantry was about a kilometre away in front of the English. They took up their positions on a narrow strip of land between Agincourt and Tramecourt. The commanders, Marshal Boucicaut and the Constable of France, Charles d'Albret, drew up their men in three ranks with the infantry and crossbowmen in the front two lines and the cavalry behind them. But on the morning of October 25, chaos broke out. As one chronicler wrote, "all the cavalry, being noblemen, wanted to be in the front line... and they were so jealous of each other they would not listen to sense".

This pressure from the rear effectively spread the front line out far

wider than planned, with the archers and crossbowmen by now on the wings. The French were so certain of victory that the Dukes of Bourbon and Orléans and the Counts of Eu and Richemont put themselves at the head of the field together with their retinues of hundreds of knights and standard-bearers. "There seemed to be more banners in the French front line than lances in the entire English army," as one eye-witness put it.

On the English side the chaplains prayed and hymns were sung until, at 11 o'clock, Henry decided to attack. To the fanfare of trumpets and cries of "In the name of Jesus, Mary and St George", the English slowly advanced. When they were 300 metres from the French the archers stopped and knelt down. They each 'stuck a thick, wooden stake, sharpened at each end, into the ground to protect them from the enemy horses. From behind this cover they unleashed their arrows.

The French cavalry was massacred. In the ensuing fighting Henry showed outstanding courage and by early afternoon the battle was won. The French third line was in full flight and 6,000–7,000 knights lay dead, among them the Dukes of Bar, Brabant and Alençon and the Counts of Nevers and Marle. Only a few escaped, among them Boucicaut and Duke Charles of Orléans, who were taken prisoner.

By November 23 Henry was back in London where he was welcomed with unprecedented scenes of national celebration. As he entered the city, the crowds sang "England, thank God for your victory".

Less than two years later, another 10,000 English soldiers landed in Normandy without encountering any opposition. Caen fell after 17 days, and the following year, after a six-month siege, Rouen also fell. Henry had achieved his first major aim, the conquest of Normandy.

France Divided

The huge defeat by the English at Agincourt and the increasingly tyrannical government made the Armagnacs more and more unpopular. The French Queen, Isabella of Bavaria, acting for her insane husband Charles VI, tried to restrain the government. However, in 1417, she was banished. She immediately changed her allegiance to the Burgundian party and set up her court at Troyes. The following year Paris once more opened its gates to John the Fearless and, as the mob again broke out into an orgy of revenge killings, the Dauphin Charles fled the capital. Not even the continued English occupation of Normandy could stop the civil war and eventually, in 1419, the Dauphin and the Duke of Burgundy agreed to meet for talks at Montereau. The meeting ended in disaster when Charles' men assassinated John. This was all that was needed to make the Burgundians take up the English cause. Their new Duke, Philip the Good, immediately supported Henry V's claim to the French throne.

After several months of negotiations, England and Burgundy signed the Treaty of Troyes on May 21, 1420. Under the Treaty it was arranged that Henry V should marry Catherine, daughter of Charles VI and sister of the Dauphin, and upon her father's death Henry would become king of France. However, two years later, on September 1, 1422, Henry died suddenly, and only two months later Charles VI also died. Thus the nine-month-old son of Henry and Catherine was proclaimed Henry VI of England and king of France.

Besieged by the English from 1419 to 1450, Mont-Saint-Michel held out against every assault. Given provisions by the local fishermen, the little garrison under Louis d'Estouteville, turned the island into a symbol of Norman resistance to the English occupation.

France was now effectively divided into three regions. The English king, Henry VI, ruled most of Guyenne, Normandy, and all the territory from the Somme to the Loire: practically the whole of the northern half of the country. Since 1418 the government of Paris had been in the hands of Burgundian nobles and clerics, such as the chancellor Jehan Leclerc, the Bishop of Beauvais Pierre Cauchon, and the city Provost Simon Morthier. But all the military power rested in the hands of the regent, the Duke of Bedford, Henry VI's uncle. Meanwhile, Burgundy had virtually become an independent state and its troops also controlled the whole of Champagne. Under the terms of the Treaty of Troyes these troops were also pledged to support the English in their attempt to conquer the rest of France from the Dauphin Charles. Nearly half the country from the Loire valley south, including the central region of France, the Dauphiné, all of Languedoc and the city of Lyons recognised the Dauphin, although uncrowned, as Charles VII of France.

Most royal officials remained loyal to Charles, who set up his government first at Bourges and then at Poitiers. His advisors included such eminent lawyers as Jean Jouvenal and Jean de Vailly, who devoted their time to discrediting the Treaty of Troyes. They argued that "as the king, Charles VI, was not responsible for his actions, he was not able to delegate to anyone else the power to will away the throne. Thus Charles VII was the legitimate king".

The whole political situation in France had reached an impasse. The Duke of Burgundy had gained independence and was quite satisfied with this, knowing he could not gain any more for the moment. The Duke of Bedford had neither the men nor the money to conquer the rest of the kingdom, and Charles VII, despite his control of a wide area, was too lazy and weak to embark on a policy of reconquering any of the rest of the country.

English Normandy

Following its conquest in 1419, Henry V added Normandy to the lands already owned by the English throne and tried to turn it into a colony by settling Englishmen there. But the scheme failed. After Henry's death, the shrewd regent, the Duke of Bedford, discovered that it was better to leave the local Norman officials to administer the Duchy while keeping the military command in English hands.

Following the end of the fighting, the English resumed trading on the river Seine and in the Channel ports. For this reason the wealthy merchants supported the English occupations, but the local nobility was still split between the Burgundian and Armagnac factions. The English remained unpopular amongst the common people, who had not forgotten the pillaging and destruction carried out by previous English armies. The most important reason for English unpopularity was very heavy taxation. Bedford imposed taxes, port-taxes and customs-duties on the Normans. With a small occupying force of a few thousand men he could only garrison the main towns. Yet, in spite of all these difficulties, his shrewd administration and his sound economic measures made it possible for him to rule "English Normandy" in peace until his death in 1435.

Badge of the supporters of the Dauphin Charles. Between 1420 and 1450 it was worn on their clothes.

The murder of John the Fearless by the Dauphin's men, September 10, 1419, on the bridge at Montereau. (From an illuminated manuscript of Monstrelet's chronicles, fifteenth century. Bibliothèque Nationale, Paris.)

The Great Schism

also included the courts and judges who settled all types of ecclesiastical disputes. This splendid court included some 3,000 people, and the Papal palace was the scene of many glittering celebrations, both religious and secular. The greatest artists, craftsmen and merchants of the day were attracted to such a centre of wealth and influence. As Avignon became such an important commercial crossroads,

Work on the Palace of the Popes at Avignon began in 1336 on the site of the former Bishop's palace. It housed the Pope's apartments, the quarters of the Papal curia and the administrative offices of the Church. It also had a chapel and a cloister. The Papal archives were brought there from Italy. A complete fortress was constructed around the Papal buildings to protect them from military assault. The entire town, bought in 1348 by the Holy See from the Queen of Naples, consisted of cardinals' residences, convents and churches.

Towards the end of the thirteenth century the troubles of the Catholic Church increased greatly as civil war in Rome drove the Popes from the city. In 1305 the Archbishop of Bordeaux was elected Pope as Clement V. By 1309 the French king, Philip IV, had persuaded the Pope to take up residence at Avignon, just outside the land controlled by the French crown. Although Avignon was part of the kingdom of Naples at this time, it was on the banks of the river Rhone and right on the French borders. In the conflict which broke out in 1337 this proximity of the Papacy to France was to prove very important.

The Holy See, or Papal court, was the centralised government of the Church, consisting of several departments. The Camerlengo, or chamberlain, was in charge of the finances, the Chancellery included clerks and lawyers who transcribed and made known to the people all Papal documents and letters. The curia

between the Mediterranean and mainland western Europe, Florentine bankers opened branches in the city.

The new capital of Christianity soon had 30,000 inhabitants, nearly as many as London. But the upkeep of the Papal administration and the military efforts to regain the Papal States in Italy, was very expensive. Taxes were levied throughout the continent on ecclesiastical lands, bishoprics, abbeys, and parish churches. But the pro-French Popes imposed only one tenth of the normal taxes on the French crown "because of the huge cost of maintaining the kingdom". The English king, Edward III, naturally protested at this, questioning the impartiality of the Holy See while it was "captive in Avignon". In 1366, the English parliament officially protested against Papal taxes, which totalled more than five times the royal revenue. The English parliament claimed that the taxes were not spent on the Church in England but were used to pay the ransom of French prisoners of war held by the English. Nevertheless, the Popes at Avignon made serious efforts to end the Anglo-French conflict, and they were influential in bringing about several of the truces.

In 1377 the efforts of Pope Gregory XI to restore peace in the Papal States were sufficiently successful to make it possible for him to return to Rome. This was against the interests of Charles V, who was afraid France would lose a powerful ally. But the Pope died the following year and a conclave was held at Rome to elect his successor. The Italians wanted to keep the Popes – and the prosperity they brought with them – in Rome and, even though the vast majority of the cardinals were French, they elected an Italian who took the name of Urban VI. There was little doubt that the cardinals had been subjected to threats over the election and as one disillusioned French cardinal put it, "better to have elected the devil himself than be murdered"!

The new Pope soon fell out with the college of cardinals, and most of the French members fled from Rome and then elected the Archbishop of Geneva as Clement VII. Pope Clement took up residence in Avignon. This split in the church, which lasted 40 years, is known as the Great Schism of the West, with two Popes in two different cities, each recognised by different countries.

Charles V of France recognised Clement VII, as did Castile, Aragon and Scotland. After a long debate the University of Paris also supported the claims of Clement. But Urban VI was recognised by the rest of Christianity, most importantly by Hungary, Poland, Flanders, the Holy Roman Empire and England.

The two "Popes" excommunicated one another and even used military force to try to defeat each other. This failed, and there followed a long period during which both Rome and Avignon tried to find a solution to the schism. However, at the Council of Pisa in 1409, matters only got worse when a third Pope, a Greek cardinal who took the name Alexander V, was elected alongside the Roman and Avignon claimants. But the Catholic Church only recognised the Popes elected at Rome.

A Crusader's sword and shield (fourteenth century).

The enthusiasm for crusades lasted well into the fourteenth and fifteenth centuries. The Papacy continually tried to build up an army of Christian knights to reconquer the holy places from Islam. In 1336, shortly before the Hundred Years War began, Philip VI assembled a fleet for this purpose in Marseilles. But the threat from England forced him to call it off. During the conflict the many truces and cease-fires were opportunities for new attempts to preach a crusade. The last major crusade was prompted by the advance of the Turks in the Balkans. In 1396 the Christian army under John the Fearless, gathered from all parts of Western Europe. But they were defeated at Nicopolis on the shores of the Danube. In 1453 the fall of Constantinople to the Ottoman Turks caused a few princes, among them Philip the Good of Burgundy, to lead crusades against the Turks: but in vain.

Popular Faith and Beliefs

Towards the end of the fourteenth century the state of the Church led to a revival of interest in witchcraft. Having sold themselves to the devil, groups of men and women were believed to gather on the sabbath to celebrate black magic rites. The Church placed witchcraft on a level with heresy and ordered the Inquisition to root out what it called Satanism. This led to many people, suspected of witchcraft, confessing under torture before being burned at the stake. (Witches on their way to a sabbath, from a drawing preserved in the Bibliothèque Nationale, Paris.)

The Church in western Europe had reached a pitiable state of decline by the end of the fourteenth century. "Three Popes! Which is the true successor of Saint Peter?" "The anti-Christ has defeated the Church!" "The end of the world is at hand!" These were the cries of the ordinary Christians of the day, already tormented by war and now also confused by the divisions within the Church.

The clergy, to whom they should have been able to turn for guidance, could not help them. The higher ranks of priests were mostly chosen from noble families, and lived lives as splendid and remote as any lord. One of the worst abuses of the system was the accumulation of clerical offices and the land, property and income that went with them. Many bishoprics or parishes were given to one man in order that he could benefit from their revenues. It was not uncommon for a cardinal to hold as many as twenty such titles. Others preferred to seek high office in government, like Regnault de Chartres, Archbishop of Rheims, who became chancellor to Charles VII. How could such bishops run their dioceses? By 1371 the Archbishop of Lyons estimated that a quarter of his parishes suffered from not having a resident priest.

The rural village priests were often no better. They usually had to spend much of their time working as clerks or farmers for the local lord, in order to make enough to live. They were badly paid, had been ordained without much instruction,

On the hat of this condemned man, burned at the stake, the executioner has written "heretic".

indeed many of them were hardly educated at all. One contemporary witness observed, "most priests cannot read, or at least only with great difficulty, and what they do read and preach they do not understand". Moral standards amongst the clergy in western Europe were very low, with an estimated one-third of priests in some regions not keeping their vows of celibacy. Many stories were told of priests who lived like any other peasants, drinking, dancing, gaming and ignoring their parish duties.

As a result, many people were so lacking in proper religious instruction that they turned for help to any popular cult, which might promise miraculous help from the Virgin Mary or the saints. The state of the Church, and scandals about it, eventually led to efforts to reform it. In England, an Oxford theologian, John Wycliff, who was a royal advisor in the disputes with the Avignon Popes, advocated the confiscation of all church property and its transfer to the state. His ideas spread from England across Europe where, in Prague, the scholar John Huss became their most famous defender.

48

The Council of Constance, in 1417, finally resulted in the election of a Pope accepted by all sides; Pope Martin V. But unity was only restored at the cost of many concessions to the Church in different countries. An important example of this was the Pragmatic Sanction of Bourges in 1438. This assembly of French clergy, brought together by Charles VII, reduced Papal power throughout the country by giving "the king or royal princes the right to intervene in ecclesiastical appointments, in order to ensure that they always went to the most worthy and devout candidates".

Villagers at Mass in the fifteenth century. The parish church was both a place of worship and the main meeting place for the local Christian community.

The Universities

In the university schools both study and teaching were predominantly oral and students relied heavily upon their own memory. They seldom wrote much and anyway books, quills and parchment were scarce, and used only by the richer clerks. The cost of fees, lodgings and giving dinners for the tutors made studying very expensive. Many students lodged with their tutors, who in their joint roles of tutor and landlord made a better profit out of their pupils.

"In accepting or rejecting ideas we should not be swayed by whether we like or dislike the person proposing them but solely by the truth of their argument. As Aristotle has told us, we should therefore love both those with whom we agree and disagree as long as they are trying to find the truth."

"But, Master, which of the two should we choose?"

"The doctor of the Church, Saint Thomas, tells us in this text that we should follow that of which we can be most certain."

In this typical scene from a mediaeval university lecture, the master would make a commentary on the works of Saint Thomas Aquinas. Like his students, he spoke in Latin, the universal language which allowed him to be easily understood in Paris, Naples, Oxford or wherever he lectured.

The main subjects taught were arithmetic, grammar and especially rhetoric – the art of speaking – and dialectic – the art of arguing and debating. The main writers studied were the ancient Greek philosophers such as Aristotle; Latin poets like Ovid and Virgil; and Christian thinkers and philosphers such as Saint Augustine and Saint Thomas Aquinas. Various theological compositions would also be included in the curriculum. By the fifteenth century this system of thought and reasoning had developed into a formal question-and-answer process in which a student would first ask, "Well, which is the correct teaching?" His master would reply, "That which is as close to the truth as we can get".

Studies were long; by the age of 22 the student, after three or four years of study, could have gained a first degree. But it could take seven or eight years to be good enough to get a well paid position: a career in the Church, or as a civil servant in a town or a high-

ranking nobleman. To be able to pay for these studies a student often had first of all to obtain an ecclesiastical office, such as becoming a cathedral canon or parish priest. He then had to study instead of carrying out the religious duties for which he was paid. Those who remained laymen might be sponsored by a nobleman or village schoolmaster for whom they would be expected to work after finishing their studies.

With some exceptions the status of a student, or clerks as they were often called, was a privileged one. He was exempted from paying state or Church taxes, and could claim the protection of the Church. Of the 4,000 students registered at Paris in 1400 and the 1,500 at Oxford and Cambridge, many joined merely to obtain these privileges and did not attend courses. They were full of life, great practical jokers and rowdy revellers. Consequently they were generally disliked by the townsfolk where they studied. But in both France and England the influence of the universities was enormous, as was proved in Paris where the king's officers invaded the university to arrest some students, only to be told to hand them over to their tutors.

Why did the universities have so much power? Mainly because they were indispensible to the European kingdoms whom they furnished with lawyers, scientists and every type of civil servant. In 1432 the Duke of Bedford founded the University of Caen, in Normandy, to educate local officials so that they could administer the English occupied province. Every university claimed that it was answerable to the Pope alone and so its theological judgements were usually accepted as correct. As the schism progressed Paris University upheld the cause of its protectors, the Burgundians. So in 1431 the English had no trouble in finding theologians from Paris to argue in favour of the condemnation of Joan of Arc as she was an enemy of Burgundy. Both in England and France the universities played an active part in the conduct of the Hundred Years War.

An Unruly Poet

On January 5, 1463, a man lay in the condemned cell at Châtelet prison in Paris. At the age of 32 François de Montcorbier, known as François Villon, had been sentenced to hang for burglary and brawling.

This brilliant man, following his studies at Paris University, wasted his life in going to taverns and brothels, and above all keeping company with vagabonds and thieves, whom he eventually joined. Nevertheless, the rowdy student turned into a great poet. Villon wrote about the people he knew. A prostitute was the heroine of this *Ballade of Fat Margot*, vagabonds and thieves were the subjects of *The Lesson of the Lost Children* and one of his close drinking friends had the poem *A Prayer for Master Jean Cotard* dedicated to him. His two *Testaments* attacked such contemporaries as a woman who had betrayed him, middle-class hypocrites and a sly innkeeper. But what haunted Villon's work most was the sense of time rushing past: "Where are the snows of yesteryear?", is the refrain from *The Ballade of the Ladies of Bygone Days*.

His sentence was reduced to ten years exile. From the terrible experiences of this, the poet produced *The Ballade of the Hanged Men*, which reflected his own great sense of loss of dignity.

Magdalen College, Oxford. Founded in the twelfth and fourteenth centuries, university colleges like those at Oxford and Cambridge or the Sorbonne in Paris, were originally intended to help poor students. They would be housed, clothed, have access to excellent libraries and in general receive a high standard of education.

Seal of the University of Paris, fourteenth-fifteenth centuries.

51

Joan of Arc

A French sallet – a kind of helmet, about 1430. It had a movable visor and a beaver – armour covering the chin and neck. Joan of Arc probably wore this type of head armour which was very popular at the time and far lighter than the old-style helmet. (Musée de l'Armée, Paris.)

In March 1429 bishops and theologians assembled at Poitiers to cross-examine a young girl of seventeen. Her name was Joan of Arc and she came from the Vaucouleurs area between Champagne and Lorraine. This small area of Burgundian territory had remained loyal to the Dauphin. A few days earlier she had arrived at Chinon in search of the man she called "the noble Dauphin" to tell him that God had sent her. Her mission was to to seek out "the true heir and son of the king" and urge him to put an end to "the misery of the kingdom of France" by expelling the English.

Was she an imposter or a genuine visionary? Were the voices which she claimed to hear from God or the devil? After the examination, the inquisitors were satisfied. Joan was a good and true Christian.

Charles VII's court was divided in its advice, some telling him she was just an adventuress but others, like the theologian Jean Gerson, urging him to accept "the divine help which had so

clearly been sent to him". Charles had nothing to lose in listening to her as his situation was so critical: the town of Orléans, which commanded the whole of the Loire valley, was besieged and if it fell the southern half of the country would be opened up to the English.

Charles accordingly put Joan in charge of a force sent to relieve the town and gave her a full military uniform. Joan marched on Orléans and met with astounding success. After harrassing the siege ramparts around the town she forced Lords Suffolk and Talbot to raise the siege on May 8, 1429, and she entered Orléans in triumph. This was followed by the defeat of the English at the battle of Patay the following month, where Talbot was taken prisoner.

Despite these great victories the royal court was still slow to take Joan's advice and march on Rheims to crown Charles king officially. It was important for the Maid, as she was now called, that Charles should be crowned and consecrated as king and take the coronation oath so that no one could dispute his legitimate claim to the throne. But several military leaders took her side and set off for Rheims without the Dauphin. Among them were the lords La Hire, Dunois – bastard son of Louis of Orléans – and Richemont. A force of some 12,000 men set out and captured the Burgundian garrisons at Troyes and Chalons-sur-Marne. On July 17, 1429, Charles VII was crowned in Rheims Cathedral. Joan, bearing her standard, which had inspired the military revival, was deservedly given the place of honour next to him.

The Treaty of Troyes was immediately revoked. More than two years later the hastily arranged coronation of Henry VI took place in Paris, but failed to threaten Charles who, by this time, was recognised as the sole lawful king of France. Immediately after his coronation Joan advised Charles to march on Paris and recapture the capital. But Paris was still in Burgundian hands, and Charles' advisers were divided: some, like the

The only contemporary drawing of Joan of Arc which has survived to the present day. The small pen drawing is in the margin of the register of the Paris parliament for May 1429, kept in the national archives. Although Joan is depicted in women's clothes and with long hair she can be clearly identified by her sword and standard.

Duke of Alençon, remained faithful supporters of Joan. The opposing faction was all for making peace with Philip the Good of Burgundy and thus having only the English to fight. Consequently Joan's attack on Paris on September 8, 1429 failed, and she herself was wounded.

After another defeat at La Charité-sur-Loire Joan was captured by the Burgundians at Compiègne on May 24, 1430. Duke Philip sold his prisoner to the Duke of Bedford for 10,000 gold crowns, and she was imprisoned in Rouen castle. Throughout this time Charles VII never made the slightest effort to help her.

Her capture was a stroke of luck for the English. They now tried to prove that she was a sorceress, who had bewitched the Dauphin Charles, so that they could still claim that God was on their side. The University of Paris was prepared to support her trial for "crimes which reeked of heresy". The main inquisitor was Bishop Cauchon of Beauvais, whose pro-Burgundian diocese had fallen to royalist forces and who had been forced to flee to Rouen.

Joan was accused of idolatry and devil worship. Bishop Cauchon was not interested in establishing the truth but only in finding the Maid guilty, as she was a supporter of Charles and the Armagnacs. But she answered her inquisitors directly and fearlessly. Asked, "Does God hate the English?" she replied, "I have no idea. But I do know that they will be hounded out of France, except for those that die here".

Worn down by her inquisitors and threatened with torture, Joan recanted, but immediately changed her mind and insisted that she had been sent by God. The court pronounced her a "relapsed heretic", condemning her to death. She was burned alive at the stake on May 30, 1431.

But all the Anglo-Burgundian alliance had achieved was to give France a martyr: the figurehead it needed to assure the liberation of the kingdom.

Arriving from Vaucouleurs in March 1429, Joan of Arc presented herself at the Chateau de Chinon where Charles VII was staying. She was made to wait a long time before being admitted to the main hall where Charles mingled with his courtiers, dressed like any other nobleman. But Joan recognised him immediately and addressed him as "the noble Dauphin". From this moment Charles believed in her.

Charles the Victorious

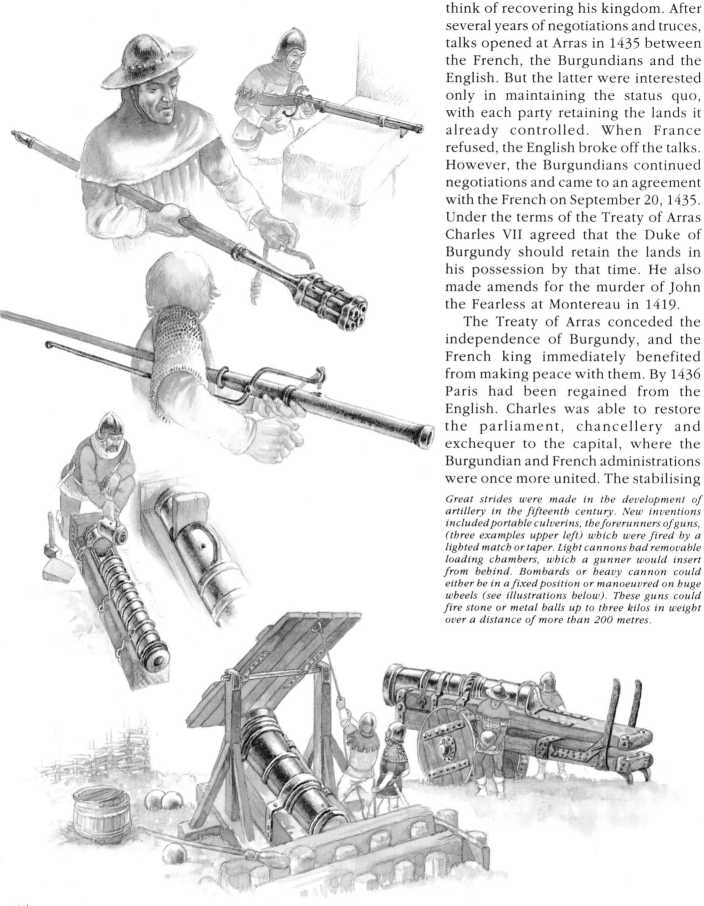

Charles VII and his ministers soon realised that a peace agreement between France and Burgundy was essential before the king could think of recovering his kingdom. After several years of negotiations and truces, talks opened at Arras in 1435 between the French, the Burgundians and the English. But the latter were interested only in maintaining the status quo, with each party retaining the lands it already controlled. When France refused, the English broke off the talks. However, the Burgundians continued negotiations and came to an agreement with the French on September 20, 1435. Under the terms of the Treaty of Arras Charles VII agreed that the Duke of Burgundy should retain the lands in his possession by that time. He also made amends for the murder of John the Fearless at Montereau in 1419.

The Treaty of Arras conceded the independence of Burgundy, and the French king immediately benefited from making peace with them. By 1436 Paris had been regained from the English. Charles was able to restore the parliament, chancellery and exchequer to the capital, where the Burgundian and French administrations were once more united. The stabilising

Great strides were made in the development of artillery in the fifteenth century. New inventions included portable culverins, the forerunners of guns, (three examples upper left) which were fired by a lighted match or taper. Light cannons had removable loading chambers, which a gunner would insert from behind. Bombards or heavy cannon could either be in a fixed position or manoeuvred on huge wheels (see illustrations below). These guns could fire stone or metal balls up to three kilos in weight over a distance of more than 200 metres.

of the economy also enabled the king to rebuild his army. But the process of reconquest was slow, disorganised and delayed by personal quarrels amongst Charles' followers.

In 1442 the king himself led a force into Guyenne but won back only a few fortresses. A truce was finally agreed in 1444 and held for a further four years. For the English, the loss of Burgundian support and the military reverses led to sharp differences of opinion in London. The Duke of Suffolk was in favour of reaching a peaceful settlement, but Duke Humphrey of Gloucester and the majority of parliament wanted to hold on to the continental possessions at all costs. However, they did not seem to realise that by now the French had the upper hand. Charles was enlarging his army month by month and at the start of 1449 launched a new offensive in Normandy. Thanks largely to his powerful artillery, he overran the fortresses in the Seine valley and entered Rouen on November 20.

A small English force under Thomas Kyriel landed at Cherbourg on March 15, 1450 and attacked the French a month later at Formigny near Bayeux. The French artillery forced the English to come out from their entrenchments and fight in the open, and the arrival of more troops under the Constable, Richemont, decided the battle. The English were beaten and Normandy fell to the French in the summer of 1450.

Military operations resumed in Guyenne, and Dunois blockaded Bordeaux in June 1451. The new French administration in the city was cruel and repressive and angered the people just as much as the cutting off of their profitable trade with England. In October 1452, an English force of only 5,000 soldiers landed in the Médoc region. Under the vigorous leadership of John Talbot, Earl of Shrewsbury, who was over 80, Bordeaux and much of the province was recaptured. Charles was now forced to mount a new campaign which led to the last great battle of the conflict. The French attacked Castillon, east of Bordeaux, on July 17, 1453. Jean Bureau's new and sophisticated artillery shattered the English cavalry, and Breton units attacked the flanks to win the battle. Talbot died bravely leading the charge. Within the next few weeks the whole of Guyenne was recaptured and a heavy tax imposed upon Bordeaux for its disloyalty and rebellion.

Charles VII, henceforth known as the Victorious, had regained his kingdom. Only a few small areas, such as the town of Calais, remained in English hands. By this time neither country could afford to launch any new military operations.

A cavalryman of Charles VII's Companies of Ordnance, about 1450. The large army corps, established in 1439, comprised cavalry units each made up of 100 lances. A lance consisted of one heavily armed cavalry officer and five mounted soldiers. From then on the the royal army controlled the recruitment, equipment and regular pay of the king's soldiers and by 1444 he had an army of more than 10,000 men. Recruitment continued throughout the truces until it had reached 15,000 men by 1447. In 1448 a new corps of "free archers" was formed and organised along the same lines as the cavalry and infantry units.

Rebuilding the Kingdoms

By 1440 in Normandy, Quercy, Burgundy and the Valois, villages and all the surrounding countryside lay deserted. In 1448 Limoges had only 15 inhabitants. The plague, war, fear of marauding mercenaries and crippling taxation had almost totally ruined France. In England, too, bands of outlaws roamed the countryside and took refuge in the forests. Between 1320 and 1450 Europe is estimated to have lost two-thirds of its population.

From 1450 onwards the precarious peace between France and England slowly became more secure. So many treaties and truces had failed before, however, that both sides were still wary of each other. Under these conditions the rebuilding of France was slow and progress varied from region to region.

But by hard work and persistence the peasants gradually improved their lifestyle. By 1485 the total area of cultivated land had returned to that of the period from 1300–1315. The increase in agricultural production resulted in the peasants having better working conditions, tools and equipment. The size of the population had dropped dramatically, so more food was available for each family. Some were even able to make money by selling their surplus crops, dairy produce, fruit and wine at the local village markets. Others sold woollen or linen cloth they had made on their own farms. Near the large towns the luckier farmers could give up growing cereal crops and turn to the more profitable business of raising cattle, as their land was protected by the town militia.

Although England had not had its countryside and towns laid waste by the Hundred Years War, it had suffered economically. A large percentage of the national wealth had been spent on the fighting and the army had taken a big proportion of the available manpower. With the return of peace the value of arable land increased. There was a growth in sheep farming; some of the wool, which in earlier years had been sent to the Continent, now stayed at home. Cloth was manufactured in England, in towns such as Coventry and Ludlow. The end of the fighting in the Channel opened up sea trade once again to English "Merchant Adventurers". These private traders sailed from London, Bristol and Southampton to all parts of Europe, from the Baltic to the Mediterranean. They exported English wood, wine, cloth and tin.

But the commercial scene in France was quite different. More than a century of war had closed the great trade routes through the country, both on land and sea. The Italian, German and Flemish merchants had fled the country and set up their businesses in Antwerp, Bruges, Frankfurt or Geneva. These were now the market centres for luxury goods such as silks, spices and precious metals. With the exception of Lyons, the process of national reconstruction did not bring any immediate international economic benefits with it.

Thus, as the fifteenth century drew to a close, France was not in a position to take part in the great age of discoveries in the New World which was just beginning.

By 1460 in most parts of France the nobles, at enormous cost, rebuilt farms, windmills, barns and market halls. The peasants started to reclaim the land and cultivate the better plots once more. But at first they lacked the manpower to be really efficient and their hard work produced only small returns. However, with the return of peace the birth rate increased dramatically and things started to improve.

A Good Business Deal

On January 12, 1472, Philippot Honffroy, a townsman from Neubourg in upper Normandy, rented two plots of land form the local lord. They were situated at Epégard, a few kilometres from the town. One plot had previously been rented by a Philippot Bésuquet, but he had disappeared. None of the locals could remember who had held the tenancy of the second plot. The land, which was by now covered in scrub, gorse, bushes and rubble was accordingly handed back to the lord of Neubourg. The previous rent had been 43 sous per year plus five young cockerels.

Honffroy got them for only 30 sous per annum, but the lease contained a clause which stipulated that "the tenant shall work and cultivate the said land". Honffroy never intended to work the land himself. He first cleared the plots and then rented them out as farmland, to local peasants, on nine-year leases. There was little doubt that his annual income from them was far greater than the 30 sous he had to pay the lord in Neubourg.

A good business deal in Paris, or the acquisition of a profitable cargo at Rouen might have brought him in a higher short-term return, but it would have been more risky. His renting of the two pieces of land was a much sounder long-term investment.

Haunted by the Fear of Death

"O miserable and bitter life! Come boiling heat or freezing cold, war, death and famine plague us day and night", wrote the French poet Jehan Meschinot in 1450. The years of war had left its mark on society. Men and women alike had become used to so many different forms of death over the centuries, in an age when a third of children died in infancy and anyone over fifty was considered an old man. Meschinot went on to add "unhappiness hangs over our poor bodies whose lifespan is so short".

But in the fourteenth and fifteenth centuries the popular vision of death itself had taken on a new horror with epidemics, wars and massacres. No longer was it the peaceful rest which was the reward of a fruitful life. Men saw it as a sickness, a suffering: "no matter how you die, death is painful", wrote François Villon. People were obsessed with the idea of the decay of mortal remains which they saw all round them. "Soon you will be just like me, a stinking corpse riddled with worms", was the epitaph on the tomb of a cardinal who died in 1402.

The idea of death as the destroyer of all beauty dominated the work of many artists, notably the Flemish master Hieronymus Bosch. His late fifteenth century paintings were filled with pictures of grimacing demons and skeletons in the shape of shells being eaten away by hideous monsters and vermin. The invention of the printing press and the resulting reproduction of wood engravings started a wide circulation of this type of art from 1450 onwards. Even the Church did little to console the faithful.

In the fifteenth century religious plays were often staged in cathedral squares. These included re-enactments of Christ's Passion, scenes from the Apocalypse and, above all, the torments of hell.

Many preachers spent far more time in describing the apocalypse, the last judgement, and the torments of hell-fire rather than reminding people of the promise of Heaven and eternal life.

Fear of the Last Judgement

Typical of the preachers of the time was Saint Vincent Ferrer, a Spanish Dominican friar, who travelled throughout Spain, France and northern Italy. Everywhere he was in great demand and was greeted with civic pomp by aldermen and burgesses. Enormous crowds assembled to hear him preach. "Good people! The day of judgement is at hand! Beware the wrath of God! Repent before it is too late!" His words were received with great enthusiasm as he called on the people to burn anti-religious pictures and books, the symbols of a decadent society. In cathedrals and churches the traditional gentle statues and frescoes of the Virgin and Child from the thirteenth century were being replaced by the new fashion in sculptures and paintings of the *Pietà*, the mother of Christ weeping over the dead body of her son.

The constant presence of death, the political and religious turmoil and the general feeling of insecurity produced a society which relished violence in all its forms. Violence of feelings was shown as well, as at the Treaty of Arras

in 1435 when the delegates, with impassioned speeches, reduced the whole assembly to tears; or when, in 1347, Edward III's queen threw herself at his feet and wept, begging for mercy for the condemned burghers of Calais. Violence was all too common in public spectacles: in London huge crowds gathered to watch thieves being hanged; in 1425, in Paris, a public amusement included a fight in which four blind men were pitted against a wild pig.

But this brutal society could turn suddenly from cruelty to kindness. In the worst years of the civil war in France a short truce, in 1418, was marked by a group of people who washed the Church of Saint Eustache with rose water. Sometimes people gave way to despair. "Would to God I had died as young", cried Philip the Good on learning of the death of his son. "I want nothing now but death", wrote Meschinot some fifty years later.

But life went on. Around 1465 an anonymous playwright wrote *The Farce of Master Pathelin*, a comedy which ridiculed a rich draper. At the same time printing houses were springing up all over Europe. In Holland, on the banks of the Rhine, scholars were already translating the works of the ancient Greeks and Romans and beginning to study the forces and origins of the universe. This century also saw the birth of Humanism, which reached its height in the sixteenth century.

The dance of death was a popular theme during the late Middle Ages. In churches and graveyards throughout Europe, notably the Church of the Divine Throne in Auvergne and the Cemetery of the Holy Innocents in Paris, frescoes depicted the same haunting scene: rattling skeletons leading men, women, children, old and young alike to their last resting place. This was a horrific spectacle for the people of those days but also a reminder of man's equality in the eyes of God. The same fate awaited everyone – kings, bishops, knights, beggars or outlaws.

The End of the War

Louis XI and Edward IV met for talks at Picquigny on August 29, 1475. Both remembered that, at a similar meeting in 1419, John the Fearless had been murdered on the bridge at Montereau. This time the French king had a wooden bridge built over the Somme with a strong trellis fixed across it.

After the English forces had finally left France the threat of a resumption of hostilities still remained. No treaty had been signed and Henry VI still called himself "King of France and England". Some groups in England still hoped to fight back. But, on top of the military defeats and the loss of his continental possessions, Henry was threatened by domestic struggles for power.

Matters had come to a head between the families of York and Lancaster. The Yorkists claimed that the Lancastrians had usurped the throne some 50 years earlier. The English barons saw in this dynastic conflict the chance to regain much of the individual power, land and money that they had lost by having to withdraw from France. They soon took sides: either with the red rose of Lancaster, the supporters of King Henry VI, or

the white rose of York, led by the Earl of Warwick.

After eight years of bitter civil war, named the Wars of the Roses, the Yorkists triumphed. In 1461 the Duke of York deposed Henry VI, and was crowned as Edward IV. The new king was now free to turn his military attention to France.

At the same time things were not going well for the French monarchy. The most powerful overlords paid little attention to royal authority, especially the Dukes of Anjou, Bourbon, Brittany and above all Burgundy. The truce between the houses of Burgundy and Valois was nothing but a memory. The Duchy of Burgundy sought complete independence and, as the chronicler Chastellain put it, "It had developed its own national culture which was totally un-French". Following the death of Charles VII, in 1461, Burgundy led a coalition which opposed the power of the French throne. The most important feudal lords called for a complete reform of government. In the name of the "Common Good", they represented themselves as defenders of provincial freedom against the taxes imposed by central government. The new king, Louis XI, saw the prospect of a new Anglo-Burgundian alliance, leading to war, looming before him.

But Louis, who according to the chronicler Philippe de Commynes, was "the cleverest man alive at getting himself out of a tight corner", anticipated the danger. First he arranged talks with the English, then in 1465 he settled the dispute of the "Common Good" by making a few wisely chosen concessions. But the threat arose again when Edward IV allied himself to Brittany and Castile and gave his sister in marriage to the new Duke of Burgundy, Charles the Bold, in 1468. Having thus strengthened his position, the English king made no secret of his intention to invade France and regain the lands of his ancestors. Louis then brought off an important diplomatic coup, persuading Warwick "the kingmaker" to change sides and support the Lancastrians.

In 1470, with French support and French money, Richard Neville, Earl of Warwick, was able to free Henry VI from imprisonment in the Tower and put him back on the throne. The newly-restored king could refuse Warwick nothing, and what Warwick asked for was help in destroying Burgundy. As one writer, Thomas Basin, put it, "The two kings (Henry VI and Louis XI) were united in their deep-seated hatred of the house of Burgundy".

But the plan immediately crumbled when Edward IV, supported by his brother-in-law, Charles the Bold, won back the English crown in April 1471, at the battle of Barnet, in which the Earl of Warwick was killed. Henry VI was then assassinated. This secured Edward IV as king, and fighting ceased until his death in 1482. This left the Anglo-Burgundian alliance stronger than ever and Edward began to prepare for a new invasion of France. Charles the Bold had already started an offensive in the north of France. The two men planned to invade and then divide France between them. Edward was to travel to Rheims, where he would be crowned.

But when Edward landed at Calais in July 1475, with 20,000 men, he learned that Charles had set off eastwards to carry his campaign into the Rhineland. None of the help promised to the English king was forthcoming from any other French nobles. Isolated and unsure of the outcome of any military engagement the English king preferred to negotiate a peaceful settlement with France. By this time King Louis, faced with internal political problems of his own, felt exactly the same. Neither was willing to risk another war. When they met, on August 29, 1475, at Picquigny on the Somme, it was to discuss a peace settlement. A seven-year truce was signed and the French king paid the expenses of the English expeditionary force, on condition it returned home. Edward did not formally renounce his claim to the French crown, and insisted on retaining Calais. But although no permanent peace treaty was ever signed no further invasions of France were attempted and the war had at last come to an end.

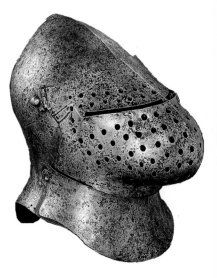

A large heavy bassinet, dated about 1450. (Musée de l'Armée, Paris.)

A sword, dated about 1400. (Musée de l'Armée, Paris.)

The Changing Role of the Monarchy

The imposing castle fortress of the Tower of London was built between the eleventh and fifteenth centuries and stood as a symbol of the power of the monarchy. This fortified palace was a favourite royal residence in mediaeval times and also a gaol for political prisoners. During the Hundred Years War many important French prisoners were held there. These included King John II in the fourteenth century and Charles, Duke of Orleans, in the following century.

By about 1350 several barons were still powerful enough to be able to afford to build their own siege engines, catapaults or mobile battering rams. The only experts they needed were a surveyor, a carpenter and some good woodcutters. A hundred years later the use of artillery demanded different skills to provide the guns and a stockpile of ammunition for them. Explosives experts, workers skilled in making cannons and specially trained gunners were all essential to modern warfare. As well as weapons becoming more sophisticated, standing armies numbered thousands of men who had to be paid, fed and equipped. The enormous cost of all this meant that it was only the major powers such as England, France and Burgundy which could afford to maintain standing armies.

Each side tried to increase the efficiency of its administration, especially in the field of tax collection and public spending. In the fourteenth century in France the old feudal system of dues was gradually increased by royal taxes which, by 1383, were a vital part of the economy. But it was indirect taxation which was the main source of revenue in both Paris and London. In 1341 Philip VI introduced in France the *gabelle*, or salt tax, while Edward III and his successors imposed customs duties and taxes on wool exports. Such measures were not popular and were not always easy to enforce.

In both countries the monarchy became more and more involved in political and religious disputes. The kings were even prepared to revive old laws to support their claims. For example, in the fourteenth century, to justify opposing the claims of Edward III, Charles V revived the Salic law – the law under which succession to the throne cannot be claimed through the female line. About 1425 the English nailed illustrated family trees to the doors of churches in Northern France to show how Henry VI was descended from Saint Louis (IX) and was thus the lawful king of France.

In times of war the monarchy made every effort to increase its power at the expense of parliament, and greater executive scope was given to the royal councils. The great legal writers and lawyers of the time of Philip IV (1285-1314) stressed the idea that the main responsibility of the king was to dispense justice. By 1310 "The king is the judge in his own kingdom", was already an accepted maxim. This implied that the monarch had to be wise, fair and impartial and look after the welfare of all his subjects. Sixty years later, the lawyers of Charles V added the stipulation that the king's power came "from the wishes and

with the consent of the people", and that "he should recognise no higher temporal sovereign than himself".

In both England and France the person of the king gradually became identified with the country itself. This was why the French remained faithful to John the Good after his capture. In their turn, the English had abandoned the use of French in everyday speech.

All these factors helped to make the two peoples conscious of their national identities. Ballads and literature, as the poems of Geoffrey Chaucer (1340-1400) show, played a large part in this process. In the early fourteenth century poetry was primarily concerned with chivalry and courtly love. But by the end of the century the *Canterbury Tales* had given England its first major literary work, written in English, about everyday people and their lives. In France too, in 1429, the *Ballade against the English* portrayed the subjects of Henry VI as crafty, proud and interested only in milking France for whatever they could get out of it.

However, regional languages and dialects were retained. In England a man from Kent had more difficulty understanding a man from Lancashire than a Norman. So by the end of the fifteenth century, both peoples felt that they were part of a separate nation and that the figurehead of that nation was the king.

The strengthening and widening of royal power led to an enormous increase in the work of the chancellery which had to implement royal statutes and ordinances.

The hand of justice, symbol of one of the main responsibilities of the sovereign.

Stone Fortresses

A king inspecting the building of a fortress (fifteenth century miniature, Bibliobèque Nationale). Architects, stonemasons and labourers are seen busy at work. Building materials were hoisted into position by a winch or carried on hods up ramps supported by scaffolding.

As most of the military action of the Hundred Years War took place in France, by the time the fight-ing ceased the country had been covered in a net-work of new or renovated castles and fortresses. Every-where in western Europe new fortifications had appeared, but not on the same scale as in France. Imposing castles appeared, for example, in Avignon, Tarascon, Vitré, Fougères and Vincennes. To protect the Valois possessions, Louis of Orléans built a line of fortresses to guard the routes from Paris to the Burgundian lands: among them were Pierrefonds, La Ferté-Milon, Vez, Montepiloy and Crépy.

At first, because there was no time to find new materials and discover new techniques, building methods remained much the same as they had been in the thirteenth century. The first improvements to be seen were thicker walls to discourage tunnelling and to withstand the heavier projectiles that were hurled at them. Some walls, as at Ham in Picardy, were as much as ten metres thick. Architects then looked for ways to strengthen the outer walls of castles. In central France a mixture of brick and ashlaring – quarried stone joined by thin strips of timber – was used. Higher towers were built, like those at Vincennes which measured forty metres. They were often topped by high roofs out of range of any catapults or similar siege weapons.

Smaller towers were built on the outside walls to protect main gates and other entrances. In the fourteenth century drawbridges were made much easier to raise with the introduction of counterweighted beams. From 1280 onwards, the English invention of projecting

64

parapets was widely adopted. These huge overhanging stone balconies contained holes in the base through which boiling pitch and projectiles, could be dropped on attackers trying to scale the walls.

These huge fortresses were often manned by only a small, hand-picked, garrison. The soldiers were able to move at great speed from one part of the castle to another as danger threatened, thanks mainly to the internal curtain platform which encircled the walls. The proud keep still remained. Larger and more comfortably furnished than ever, it stood alone at the centre of the castle. The fortress built by Charles V at Vincennes in 1370 was described as a castle within a castle. The French king had not forgotten the experience of 1358 when Etienne Marcel was able to penetrate his royal residence in Paris and sack it.

Castles were not the only heavily defended buildings. Bridges, windmills and churches were often fortified. Some cathedrals, like Albi, had almost become castles. Towers were added to abbeys and sometimes to farms. But fortifying a town was a much more specialised and expensive procedure for the burgesses. The length of town boundaries to be defended was often considerable and economies had sometimes to be made. For instance, the ramparts at Avignon were barely eight metres high, and made out of inferior materials. Such defences could hold out against a small raiding party but not a proper siege or against artillery. The adapting of stone fortresses to withstand artillery was a slow process. The castles of the time of Louis of Orléans hardly took it into account at all. But builders knew that artillery could be used in defence as well as attack. Below the arrow slits they built

housing for cannon and other firearms on the outside of the walls. At some castles, such as Fougères, Mont-Saint-Michel and Ham, special towers were built just for artillery. The huge, narrow buildings were reinforced at ground level and had special ventilation shafts to disburse powder smoke, as well as niches in which the gunners could shelter from any falling masonry caused by the gun's explosions.

By the end of the fifteenth century cannons and mortars in general had become too powerful for the old mediaeval castles. Even so, at Salses Castle near Perpignan, the builders tried to save the fortress from the assailants' fire by surrounding the entire walls with a skirting wall to deflect the cannonballs. By this time artillery had completely revolutionised the art of fortification.

Two examples of fourteenth century military architecture: Valentrè bridge at Dahors (Lot Department) and the ramparts of Dinan Castle (Cotes-du-Nord Department).

Joan of Arc: Fact and Fiction

Joan of Arc by W. Marshall (mid-seventeenth century). This is believed to be the only English picture representing Joan of Arc "condemned for witch-craft".

From the start the role of Joan of Arc in history has been the subject of controversy. From the time of her reinstatement (1456) French writers have tended to portray her as the shepherdess sent by God to save the Valois dynasty.

Yet the Burgundian chroniclers of the period remained hostile to her and even Monstrelet, who must have met her, claimed that he could not remember doing so. The physical descriptions of Saint Joan left by her contemporaries are very vague. Most pictures of her were highly romanticised. In the first miniatures illustrating the fifteenth century chronicles she appears like a classical or Biblical heroine, recognisable only by her sword and standard. Then in the sixteenth century her image became blurred and writers, often copying each other, recounted only the highly coloured episodes of her life. During the post-Reformation wars of religion Joan was adopted in France as the patroness of the Catholic cause, while the Protestants pulled down her monument on the bridge at Orléans. From the end of the sixteenth century she was often depicted wearing a cloak and cockaded hat, the symbols of victory.

In the seventeenth century the main account of her life was contained in a 30,000-line poem by Chapelain. Entitled *The Maid*, it was dedicated, in 1656, to the Duke of Longueville, a descendant of Dunois. It was a mixture of fact and fable, written without reference to any late mediaeval texts. As for the Church, while it did not question the divine nature of Joan's mission, it remained cautious about her and would not yet begin proceedings which would lead to her being recognised as a saint.

During the eighteenth century Enlightenment, renewed interest was shown in her life-story and her memory was still honoured in Rouen and Orléans. But during this period many of the great philosophers made her the object of ridicule. Voltaire's *The Maid*, a romantic epic (1755) was a scandalous best-seller. He scoffed at her virginity and criticised her earlier biographer Chapelain for being stupid enough to take such a subject seriously.

But during the French Revolution (1789–98) and the Empire of Napoleon (1799–1815) she was once more held up as a national heroine, a daughter of France who had defeated the English. Then, with the restoration of the monarchy (1815), people began to treat her story more seriously. She had been a symbol of hope to the French Royalist party in exile, which looked back to the time when she had saved the throne in 1429. The restoration of the monarchy coincided with the upsurge in interest in Gothic art and literature throughout western Europe. Writers took a more scholarly interest in the Middle Ages, and in the process

Joan of Arc, a prisoner at Rouen, by Philippe Revoil (Musée des Beaux-Arts, Rouen). Painted in 1819, this picture sacrifices any attempt at historical accuracy in favour of a romantic portrayal of the heroine.

unearthed contemporary documents relating to her. Quicherat published the transcripts of her two trials and the great French national support for her cause.

It is estimated that between 1880 and 1930 some 500 statues of her were built in France, and

Joan at the coronation of Charles VII, a mural in the Pantheon, Paris. Painted by J. E. Lenepveu (1819-1898). In the late nineteenth century this image of the national heroine was very popular.

sympathetic biography of her in 1908. When the First World War broke out in 1914 she was invoked by the French as the symbol of national unity against the enemy and the protectress of French troops ... and for the first time of English troops as well.

Her story reached its climax in 1920 when Pope Benedict XV canonised her and she became a saint. When the Second World War broke out and France fell to the Germans in 1940, the country was again divided and both sides tried to adopt her as their patroness. The Vichy regime exhorted the French people to see her as the model of "work, the family and the motherland", while the resistance adopted her as their patroness in the struggle against the occupying forces.

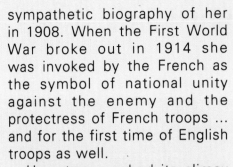

Joan at the stake. Ingrid Bergman as Joan in the 1954 film directed by Roberto Rosselini. In the twentieth century the cinema revived the story of Joan of Arc and several films about her were very successful. Some even launched new fashions in hairstyles.

historian Jules Michelet wrote a biography of her, in 1841, depicting her as a national saint.

These mediaeval documents also radically changed the artistic depictions of her. Gone were the romanticised clothes and in came more realistic portraits of her in mediaeval armour, complete with authentic weapons and her standard. The Church also began to take a serious interest in the revival of her story. In 1869 Bishop Dupanloup of Orléans asked the Papacy to start proceedings to investigate her possible beatification and canonisation. When, in the following year, during the Franco-Prussian war, France lost Joan's homeland, Lorraine, to the Germans this led to popular

she became a popular figure for engravers and copiers who mass-produced pictures, plates, and postcards of her. She became the subject of some 30 plays, notably George Bernard Shaw's *Saint Joan.*

She aroused both patriotic and religious fervour. France was ruled by an anti-clerical, republican government when, in 1909, Joan was beatified by Pope Pius X. This event was just what the Church and Monarchist parties in France needed to support their cause. But the republican authorities did not want her to be seen solely as a defender of the Church and one of their leading supporters. Anatole France, was commissioned to produce a highly

Museums, Ruins and Relics of the War

The Museum of Mediaeval Warfare at the chateau of Castelnaud (Dordogne).

Although it ended more than five hundred years ago there are still plenty of relics of the Hundred Years War both in France and England. But today there is nothing left on the plains of Crécy, Poitiers or Agincourt to suggest that large, bloody battles were ever fought there. The main relics, ruins and artefacts of the war are to be found in museums or in the great castles that have survived intact or as ruins in France, England, Belgium or Spain.

At **Langeais** in the Loire valley, the castle, which was built in 1465, is still furnished in its original style. Near Paris the **Castle of Vincennes**, built for Charles V, still has its keep and ramparts intact. **Pierrefonds**, near Compiègne in the Oise Department, was completely restored between 1857 and 1870 by the architect Violet-le-Duc. Some experts have criticised the restoration but nevertheless it shows what a fortress really looked like in the time of Louis of Orléans. He was a patron of the

arts who did not like just a stark, practical style of building. Instead he decorated windows and chimneys and even the outside of tower walls. Both Pierrefonds and La Ferté-Milon have their outside walls decorated with statues of famous figures such as Caesar, Hector or Charlemagne. This fashion for

making castles more like comfortable, attractive residences was much more widely used in England, where there was less threat from war. Good examples of it can be found at Stokesay Castle in Shropshire, Carew Castle in Pembrokeshire and Herstmonceux in Sussex. But the best English example of fifteenth century decorative additions to a fortress can be found in Saint George's Chapel at Windsor Castle. In Normandy visitors to **Mont-Saint-Michel** can see fine examples of English siege artillery. In the forecourt are two cannon and a pile of iron and stone cannonballs abandoned after the abortive siege in 1434.

Souvenirs of Saint Joan of Arc abound, especially around her home town of **Domrémy**, in the Vosges Department. The house where she was born is now a museum. At **Chinon** the old town, around the main crossroads, is very much as she would have found it in 1429. The castle still dominates the scene as it did when she met the Dauphin there. The house where

she stayed in **Orléans** in April and May of 1429 was badly damaged in 1940. It has been restored and now houses an exhibition of her travels and the campaign in which she liberated the town.

Many towns still have their late mediaeval fortifications. In England a good example is **York**, and in France **Dinan** and **Fougères**. In Belgium, the town hall at **Bruges** dates from the fourteenth century as do many of the surrounding churches and houses. **Ghent** is one of the best surviving monuments to the great commercial cities of the Middle Ages. Its belfry, castle (the residence of the Counts of Flanders), embankments, vegetable market and meat market all date from the fifteenth century. In Italy, **Florence** is one vast museum dominated by the tall palace tower, built in the fourteenth century. The whole place evokes the spirit of everyday life in a mediaeval city.

There are exhibits from the Hundred Years War in many museums. The **Tower of London** houses one of the best collections of fourteenth and fifteenth century armour and weapons in the world. This includes a superb example of equestrian armour. Other weapons from the Middle Ages can be found in the **Imperial War Museum**. The famous Musée de l'Armée in **Paris**, in the Hotel des Invalides, has many weapons from the period, including five huge artillery pieces left behind by the English after the siege of Meaux in 1422.

The fortress of **Castelnaud** in the Dordogne, built between the twelfth and sixteenth centuries, houses a museum of mediaeval warfare. It includes some excellent reconstructions of catapaults, siege weapons and complete defence systems typical of those used in the Hundred Years War.

Chronology

1324
Annexation of the Duchy of Guyenne

June 6, 1329
Edward III pays homage to Philip VI

May 24, 1337
Second annexation of Guyenne

November 1337
Edward III declares war

June 24, 1340
Naval battle of Sluys

August 24, 1346
Battle of Crécy

August 4, 1347
Calais falls to the English

1348-1352
The Black Death

September 19, 1356
Battle of Poitiers

February-July 1358
Etienne Marcel's revolt in Paris

May 1358-June 1360
Peasant uprisings in France

1360
Anglo-French Treaty of Brétigny and its ratification at Calais

May 16, 1364
Battle of Cocherel

1367
Battle of Najera

October 1370
Du Guesclin made Constable of France

1378
Start of the Great Schism of the West

1381
Peasants' Revolt under Wat Tyler

1399
Henry of Lancaster overthrows Richard II

November 23, 1407
Louis of Orléans assassinated in Paris 1413 Cabochien riots in Paris

October 25, 1415
Battle of Agincourt

1417
End of the Great Schism

September 10, 1419
John the Fearless assassinated at Montereau

May 21, 1420
Treaty of Troyes

May 8, 1429
Orléans recaptured by the French

May 30, 1431
Joan of Arc burned at the stake at Rouen

September 20, 1435
Franco-Bugundian Treaty of Arras

1436
Charles VII re-enters Paris

April 15, 1450
Battle of Formigny

1453
Start of the Wars of the Roses

July 17, 1453
Battle of Castillon

August 29, 1475
Anglo-French Treaty of Picquigny

Glossary

Beatificaton The first stage in the process of making someone a Saint. After beatification they are known as "Blessed".

Canonisation The final stage in the process of making someone a saint in the Roman Catholic Church.

Celibacy The state of being unmarried.

Cog A three-masted, wooden ship with square sails.

Conclave The meeting at which cardinals elect a new Pope. The word comes from the closed room in which they meet.

Crown The governing power of a king or queen; derived from the crown that they wear.

Curia The Papal court and the people who work in it. It includes the main judicial and administrative bodies of the Roman Catholic Church and is run by the Pope.

Dynasty A family of rulers, each ruler inheriting his title and power.

Estates General Also known as the States General. A meeting of representatives of the three divisions of French society which advised the king. The three estates were made up of the lords spiritual (clergy), the lords temporal (nobility) and the middle classes.

Excommunicate To suspend a person from membership of the Church, especially receiving the sacraments such as Holy Communion.

Fief Land granted to a person in return for promises of loyalty and service. A person granted a fief could collect rents and revenues from it and administer justice there.

Homage When a man paid homage he knelt and placed his hands inside those of his overlord's, swearing loyalty and faithful service. The overlord in return swore to protect his man.

Mercenary A hired soldier. One with no particular allegiance except to those who paid him for fighting. Many mercenaries changed sides in mid-campaign.

Militia A military force, usually raised among the civilian population, to protect its own town or region.

Overlord The person who owned land, received revenues from it and dispensed justice in a territory. He had a duty to protect his people and they to serve him.

Papacy The office of being Pope.

Prelate A high-ranking church official such as a bishop or cardinal.

Provost In France, a high-ranking official in town government, equivalent to a mayor.

Sacred College The body of cardinals of the Roman Catholic Church. The senior advisors to the Pope.

Schism A split within a church due to such violent disagreement that separate factions are created.

Seneschal An officer, or steward of a palace or great house, responsible for the smooth running of the domestic side of life.

Tithes A tax paid to civil or church authorities which amounted to one tenth of the produce of the land or a person's labour.

Usurp To sieze power unlawfully.

Index